Detachments

If It Is Not by Loving, It Will Be by Hurting

Jacqueline Sewell

BALBOA.
PRESS

A DIVISION OF HAY HOUSE

Balboa Press books may be ordered through booksellers or by contacting:

Balboa Press
A Division of Hay House
1663 Liberty Drive
Bloomington, IN 47403
www.balboapress.com.au
1 (877) 407-4847

Print information available on the last page.

ISBN: 978-1-5043-0649-2 (sc)
ISBN: 978-1-5043-0650-8 (e)

Balboa Press rev. date: 03/14/2017

People, most often, will not learn by example; but by undergoing the painful trials of life. Thus, in the majority of time, we will only search for any kind of spiritual help when facing some kind of suffering. JS

Introduction

The universe has its own peculiar way of shuffling our lives. When our true self, our soul, sleeps in the false reality created by the ego, by the forces of our physical body, and through it drags us into the illusions of materiality; then comes the tumult of changes restructuring our most intimate creations. Forcing us to move into a new direction that will show the path of self-awakening.

This book is my soul journey to self-discovery. Enjoy!

Chapter 1

The Beginning

I don't recall much about my infancy. All I can remember is that I was a chubby baby that became a very skinny and shy little girl. Everything I know comes from a few old photos and what my mother says in small conversations. We used to live in the northeast of Brazil and had a pretty good life. But most of what I can remember is from when I was four to five years of age. Prior to that, I have no recollection.

My mother and father did not seem to be an "in love" sort of couple, but they weren't unhappy either. Dad was a good husband and a hardworking man—a good provider, indeed. He fulfilled his manly duties well and was content with his married life. But then again, who could complain about my mother?

Although she was a little impatient with us, as Mom had already helped her mother to raise five of her siblings, she was a dedicated mother and housewife. She was a happy and strong person, a great cook, very clean and organized. To my dad, she was a solicitous wife, with a hint of a strong and fiery personality that made him laugh.

They liked to entertain. The house was always full of their friends on weekends. Dad would tell his jokes while drinking his whisky or rum and listening to his favorite Samba songs. They both enjoyed having friends over. I believe that deep down my parents really loved each other but did not know how to show it. At least not in front of us.

At bedtime my father sang lullabies to my brother and me. Dad tucked us into bed and would tell us stories, sing, or just caress our hair until we fell asleep. My father showed a calm personality and was very affectionate to us. All seemed peaceful at that time.

But things changed. Something wasn't right; their relationship was deteriorating. And one day, Dad left Mum for a younger woman. He was quickly gone, and with that, our lives changed drastically.

Dad came home only once per month, if that. He would leave some money on the table for food. There was always a fight between them, when he came over. We all were sad and in a bad financial situation because Mum did not work. She did not have anyone to leave us with. Her uncle used to live far away, her immediate family was living in the south of Brazil, and the three of us felt abandoned by Dad.

A year passed. I was five and my brother was three when Mum found out about Dad's extramarital affairs. I could not understand why he would leave her for someone else. My mother was a gorgeous lady, a beautiful person, had the biggest heart ever, and they seemed to be happy. She had a great figure and very long, straight, black hair. She had olive-bronze skin, a killer smile, and beautiful light-green eyes. Dad left her when she was just twenty-five years old, saying that she was past the due date— meaning that she was already too old, and the other one was much younger than her. Nonsense. He was blind or under some kind of spell or something. Dad was a macho type of a guy, typical from that region of Brazil.

Then, Mom decided to cut her hair short, and for the first time, went out with some neighbor friends to a carnival party. With that beauty and youth, Mum obviously would call some attention and probably found a boyfriend at the party. Well, it did not take long for Dad to find out, and that was when our whole story changed.

Chapter 2

A Living Nightmare

The scenario was very much like a horror movie. It was pouring rain that night. It had been quite a while since Dad came over to drop off some money for us. We used to live in a two-storey house, and on that night, while my mother was tucking us into bed, we suddenly heard strong bangs on the front door and a male voice screaming, "Open the door! We need to talk. We must go to my sister's house."

It was my father. He was holding a brown paper bag that was hiding a huge butcher's knife.

I believe that even before going down to open the door, Mum intuitively knew what was about to happen because she looked at us, so scared, and the color in her face just disappeared.

Mum went downstairs and opened the door. We heard my father come in and then we heard them talking. For some unknown reason, Dad was saying that we should go to his sister's house, and my mother got suspicious of that story, especially since it was late at night and pouring rain. When she saw the pack that he was holding, she tried to buy some time by asking him to close the back doors while she got us from bed and prepared to leave.

After that, all happened very quickly; time just sped up. I can only remember pieces of the puzzle of the most horrific event of my life. When Mom asked him to lock the back door, she was just trying to run away to a neighbor's house with us. She rushed us out in the middle of the rain, but he soon noticed and came running after her.

With the knife now showing in his hand, he stabbed her seven times in front of my brother and me. The first one was in her back; she fell in the middle of the street. We were all screaming and crying, calling for help. She called for help too. My brother and I were by her side the whole time, holding the tip of her purple dress. It was like my father did not see us at all, like he was possessed and blind.

All I could see was her being stabbed many times in her back. It looked like he was trying to hurt her in the heart, but she fought, and every time he stabbed her, she turned her back to him. There was blood everywhere, and the rain was washing it down the drain. This image got stuck in my mind. I will never forget that. Today I have a phobia; I cannot see a lot of blood because it gives me a sensation that I will faint.

I believe this affected my brother in different ways. He was younger than me but could remember every little detail of it. I probably blocked much of it.

My mother is a strong woman. She fought for her life the whole time. No neighbors came out, but one pregnant lady across the road came out to her veranda and screamed, "Someone, call the police!"

And I guess my dad, in his trance, heard, "Look, the police!" After that, he instantly came out of it, dropped the knife, and looked confused, like he was waking from a bad dream. He ran away, leaving us there—two kids, crying, horrified, lying beside their mother's bleeding body on the street. She was barely alive as she'd lost so much blood.

The rain eased up, and the street started to get packed with curious people. Our neighbor, our mother's friend, quickly took us from the scene.

My mother was taken to the hospital. She told us two stories that occurred on the way. She talked the whole time with the driver, and every time she spoke, blood came out of every perforation. The driver was getting very nervous that she would die in his car before getting to the hospital, so he asked her to please stay quiet.

She answered, "No way, sir. I need to talk to you, so I can make sure I am alive. I have two kids to look after."

When they got to the hospital, the doctor looked at her and said, "Lady, you must have seven lives like the cats do because you should be dead by now."

Yes, she has seven lives, all right—and more. But above all, she has willpower like no other person I have ever met in this world. My mother was fighting for her life so she wouldn't have to leave us with our dad.

The next morning, my mother's uncle (may God bless his soul), our first guardian angel in this life, came to get us from the neighbors'. We were so scared and had cried ourselves to sleep. Our uncle was like a parent to us.

While mom was in hospital, and as they did not know if she would survive, she made her uncle our legal guardian to stop the possibility of my dad trying to get us from him.

I am not sure if this would be the case in the event of her death. But back then my father knew very important people, and this was just a fear she had.

My uncle was the sweetest man ever. He used to put my head on his shoulder and sing, "Slope your little head on my shoulder and cry … tell me all your heartbroken things because who cries on my shoulder, I swear will not go away … will not leave me, because loves me." That song put me to sleep many nights. This song brings tears to my eyes, and wherever he is, he knows I always think of him with so much love and gratitude.

Every time I asked him when my mother would come back, I cried because he didn't know. But Mum was released after several months.

Dad was not imprisoned because he had influential good

friends, such as the sheriff of the city we lived in. He stayed in jail just for one night and was bailed out by friends. But believe it or not, he even had the nerve to secretly visit Mom in hospital, and once she was out, he tried to take her to court to get full custody. Thank God she won the battle.

But that wasn't only it. He tried many times to convince her to forgive and get back to him, crying and saying that he badly regretted what he did, that he did not even know how he could do such a thing. He would say that if he can't even stand up a hand to discipline his own kids—that I must say is true, he never landed a hand on us. He said he didn't not have much recollection of that night; as it was like he was possessed by something out of his control, but what motivated him to attack was actually one of mum's aunts, who had a crush on him. She poisoned his mind against Mom.

I hope this lady knows what she has done with her devious ways. The people who knew Dad up close support his story and were surprised to find out what he did to my mother. They were close friends for many years, and he has always been of a very placid nature. I guess his pride spoke too loudly and he learned his lesson.

Dad cried a lot for her forgiveness, but she never gave in. He said he loved her and that she would be the only woman in this world he would ever love, even though he was already involved with someone else. Dad mentioned that he regretted the day he left home, but it was all too late. I guess he lived with this guilt and regret for the rest of his life (My father passed away over five years ago; lonely, in his bed, with no one else but his faithful dog by his side).

My mother was determined to stay away from him and move on with her life, which is what she did. Once Mum was fully recovered, the three of us moved to the southeast of Brazil, where her parents and siblings were living.

The climate change was a big shock for all of us, as we came from a place where it was summer all year around, to where they have the four seasons in one day. Worst still, back then, their winter was really harsh. I don't like winter, so I suffered with that a lot.

Nonetheless, we tried not to think about everything, and when we arrived there, we felt relieved. The presence of my father always circling Mum was making me literally sick to my stomach. I always had the impression that he would do it all over again. Thank God for that move. That was a wise decision, as I do not believe he would have left her alone had we stayed.

By writing and reliving this horrific experience of my early life, I came to the belief that I have forgiven my father. For some reason I could never hate him. Subconsciously, my first lesson of detachment was a profound one for a young soul, as I saw everything without judgment. Although I could not understand how someone could get to the point of hurting the one he loves, who am I to judge the mind set of a person who is instigated and moved by the most primitive part of us, the ego?

Nonetheless, I realized this experience scarred me in a deeper but at the same time subtle way, one I could never admit until later in my married life. I see today that although it made me fearless to go through the sorrows of life, this event unleashed the initial phase of my creations of walls to keep the male figures away from my life, and from my heart.

Chapter 3

A Hard New Beginning

I was about to celebrate my seventh birthday, and my brother would be turning four, and a whole new world was ahead of us—mind you, not a wonderful world. Life was not easy for us. My mother, my hero, worked hard all her life to support us. Sometimes we would only see her on Sundays.

For the majority of our childhood, we were raised by my grandmother, her mum. Our nan is another strong woman, a fighter, the family matriarch, the root and pillar that supports our large family. She was a mother to seven children, and the last one grew up with us mostly like a sister because she is five years younger than me.

Life was tough, but it was a new beginning with hope, and Mum never complained. What a powerful woman!

After that, every year in August, my father used to come to see us, but every time he came over, I used to have that horrible sensation on my stomach, which made me run to the toilet many times. That was due to my mother arguing with him every single time he came to visit. She made sure to humiliate him and rub it in his face what he had done to her. It was unpleasant and quite traumatic. I eventually understood the way she chose to release her anger.

Although I was always happy to see Dad, I could not wait for

him to go away. One day, when I was nearly a teenager, I told her that her arguments with him was causing me to have the "runs" every time he was over, because it gave me the sensation that all would happen again. After that, she eased up a little—just a little.

Dad always took it on the chin but used to mention that she had a heart of steel. He knew he deserved all that. By the way, he remarried and had another three children. I have two half sisters and one half brother, with whom I have a good relationship.

Let's fast forward a little. When I was around nine, my mother fell in love again. This man helped her to raise us, but for some reason I never was very fond of him. I guess my strong sensitive nature was telling me it wouldn't work. But he stayed with us for many years, and I am grateful for him to be around at the time, as he helped us with everything, such as school, food, and clothing, and made my mother happy.

They had so much chemistry; I believe he was the love of her life. He acted like a father figure to us, and from their union, when I was eleven years old, my youngest brother was born.

I remember that day. His father was nervous and came home from the hospital to get some baby items. He said, "You know that you have a baby brother? I don't know what to name him. Do you have some ideas?"

I happily replied with a name that I liked. He also liked the sound of it but did not know how to spell it, so I wrote it for him on a piece of paper, which he put on his pocket in order to register the baby's name. He asked me how I knew to spell it, and I replied that I used to watch an American TV show that had an actor with that name.

My baby brother was like a son to me, and I loved him right away. Mum had to go back to work soon after he was born, and I had to help Nan look after him. He sometimes called me Mum when he started to talk; it was funny. He was always a happy but hungry baby. By the time he was nine months old, he was nearly my weight. My little Buddha, so big, heavy, and cute.

Chapter 4

· ·

Pressure Cooker Atonement

A round eleven years old, I got my first job selling cosmetics through a magazine. My mother could not understand how those adults would let me do that, leaving all those products and money with a child. But I was always a responsible child, and by my thirteenth year, I knew how to cook, clean, hand wash the clothes, iron, do grocery shopping, was an A-plus student, and looked after my brothers.

That was a hard life, but somehow in simple things we find happiness. We had a simple but comfortable life. Mum always worked hard, and we did not go without the necessary things.

But not all was hard work. I took time to have fun too. I liked to play volleyball on the street we lived on, and to play with my mother's makeup, pretending to be a model, with my friends. I used to make them do the catwalk and choreographed moves for us to dance to.

Amid all this fun, I went through my first atonement in life. One day, when I was playing volleyball outside, it was almost time for Mum to arrive from work. She was quite a short-fused person back then, had very little time for us as she worked long hours, and had little patience. Everything would end up in a big spanking. Whatever naughty things my brothers did, I was made responsible for it. Today I understand her reasons;

she was extremely mistreated by her father all her life, which is how she learned how to be tough.

On a certain occasion she asked me to cook beans in a pressure cooker to get dinner started. This is normal daily food in Brazil (a meal consists of beans, rice, some kind of white or red meat, and salad). But I was happily playing volleyball on the street, and forgot all about the beans.

My grandmother came running and screamed, "Girl, you forgot to cook the beans, and your mother is about to arrive. Run, you still have time!" (That is why we love our grannies; they are always covering for us.)

I quickly ran home and put the beans on to cook, but as I thought it was close to the time of her arrival, I did not take all the pressure out. Well, you can imagine what happened—it exploded on my face.

The lucky thing was that I had taken the majority of the pressure out, and I closed my eyes at that instant of explosion, so only the steam burned me (all the skin on my face fell off). It hurt like hell, an endless burning sensation, such agony.

When my stepfather and Mum got me from the hospital, I looked like a mummy, with bandage covering my whole head. My mother and middle brother cried a lot when they saw me.

The doctor told my mother that I could have plastic surgery, depending on my recovery, and that I would not be able to talk, laugh, cry, or make any facial movements until all the underneath skin dried. Otherwise, it would wrinkle, leaving me with big scars.

At that age, all my concerns were that I was going to end up ugly (I always have been vain), with a scarred face, scaring away friends and future boyfriends. But Nan and Mum were careful. Every day a lady came to my home to bless my face and help with my recovery.

One day, right before I was supposed to take off the bandage, some friends from school came over to visit. I remember them playing and trying to make me laugh. I could not hold it in anymore; that was when I felt my skin stretching. So I cried, screamed, the whole lot, expressed all the emotions I couldn't before, and my angry grandmother sent everyone home. It's funny to talk about now, but back then it was a tragedy.

The day I took off the bandages was a stressful and scary one. I looked horrible in the mirror. There were pieces of dried and burnt skin, and the places where they had fallen off was showing a new reddish-white skin—not a pretty sight.

I had already missed too many days of school and was forced to go like this and face the world. That was quite traumatic and courageous for my early teen years.

Thank God I did not need plastic surgery. With time, and a cream the doctor prescribed, together with a lot of blessings too, my skin slowly returned to normal. I was so glad that everything was over and had my old self back—less one layer of skin, of course.

Throughout my life I have had encounters with people blessing me for evil eyes - The evil eye is a curse believed to be cast by a malevolent glare, usually given to a person when they are unaware. Many cultures believe that receiving the evil eye will cause misfortune or injury (Wikipedia).

From then on I became a pretty sweet girl, although not a typical Brazilian girl in the physical sense, as I was way too skinny. But I had long and beautiful curly hair and dark olive skin.

Mum and Nan noticed that I was easily getting sick to my stomach, often with stomach pains, drowsiness, and lethargy. They used to take me to a lady on the upper street to do some healing work on me, and maybe clear out my evil eyes.

It's funny how the Brazilian catholic are; they have always mixed their religion with some afro-religion beliefs. The lady used to say to my mother that she could not understand why I always had so many evil eyes on me; she believed it was due to my beautiful hair locks.

Today I know why; I was always sensitive to energies and absorbed the bad ones. Since I was little, I used to see people's auras, but back then I thought that everyone had this ability. Naively, I attributed the light I saw to whether they had prayed that day.

I have always been around psychic events but did not know how to deal with them; I was too scared to mention them. Sometimes the auras were faint in color, and during one of those instances I told my teacher that she needed to pray more, because her light was not too good on that day. She did not understand but did not question either.

Once I was at my great-grandmother's (from Mum's dad's side) home. She used to bless little babies with branches of a powerful plant called Rue - (this plant absorbs and cleanses negative energies in the house and around people. It is commonly used in Brazil by healers.)

On this day, she went outside to get more branches of rue to bless a baby with a bad stomach ache. Prior to this, she had finished blessing another baby, and the used leaves were withering.

My great-grandmother left the baby on the middle of the bed and asked me to look after him for a second, while she grabbed some fresh rue from her backyard. When she left, I quickly took the used leafs and started praying the Holy Father prayer over the baby's stomach, asking God to pass all his pain to me, because I was older and could handle it better.

Guess what? By the time my great-grandmother came back, the baby had stopped crying and she saw me finishing my prayer. Long story short, the baby got better and I ended up with a huge bout of diarrhea!

My first healing and another detachment lesson: Do not ever ask to get other people's issues transferred to you—what is yours is yours, and what is theirs is theirs. Each and every person can handle his or her own pain. You may help heal, but do not allow illness to be released onto you. In order to heal or help others, you must detach yourself from their issues and be a clean conduit, a neutral catalyst of energies.

Chapter 5

Teen Years

During my pre-teen years, our lives were tough, but we had great times. On school holidays, my stepfather took us camping near the beach. Mum loved to camp, and although I love the beach, I never liked camping much. I always was scared of bugs and crawling animals. I am terrified of snakes and any venomous creatures.

In Brazil, when a girl turns fifteen, she is given a huge debutant party, much like the sweet sixteens in the states. But my mother could not afford to give me this party, so for the first time, I rang my father to ask for something.

I knew he was in a much better financial situation than we were, so I asked him to send me the money to organize my birthday party. He promised to send it, and even told me to start inviting my friends, because he would come over himself to dance with me.

Well, my birthday came and went and he never showed up, nor did the money. I learned my first adult lesson then—never expect anything from anyone, and if I wanted something, I would have to work for it.

So I did. I officially started working with my stepfather at age fourteen, although before that I sold cosmetics. My stepfather was a mechanic and had an office above his shops. He taught me all about office work, and with the little money he paid me, I bought clothing and shoes and paid for my dancing and modelling classes. I took some typing courses, and it was a great experience. After that, I got a real full time job as an office assistant at a small accountancy company.

I worked full time during the day and studied in high school at night. I loved my financial independence from day one; I learned well with my mother but also learned from her how to be a big spender. I have never been really good at saving money. She was generous, and so am I.

Back then, I was a shy girl who kept to herself and had pretty different views of the world and life from my family and the people around me. I was ambitious and wanted to get somewhere in life but would never step on anyone's toes to get there.

During the 1980s I became a goth, but not a radical one; I just liked the fashion and the music. So I always dressed in black, frequented dark parties, and listened to music from The Smiths, The Cure, Siouxsie and the Banshees, The Sugarcubes, Sex Pistols, Cocteau Twins, and so on.

I enjoyed my dark but innocent years. I have never been curious about drugs since I thought that would be a waste of my time, and moreover, it would hurt the values that I got from my mother. I really just enjoyed dancing to the songs from those wonderful years. I have always had eclectic tastes in music, as I also appreciated the Brazilian '80s bands, the bossa nova, and American pop music.

At heart I was a shy girl but shown a strong personality (and at the same time a lonely soul) because of the walls I subconsciously built with the opposite sex. Deep down I was very romantic. I had many platonic love experiences that made me cry a lot with those '80s ballads, but have never invested in any of those boys; I was too afraid to get rejected and hurt. To be honest, I never had a real boyfriend until I was nearly eighteen.

I kept my dream of being "someone" as my first priority, and that gave me a reason to not care much about boys. Besides, I was never the typical Brazilian stereotype of the curvy and extroverted girl; my shyness camouflaged my lack of confidence with the guys—it made me think that it was best for me to invest in myself and let life bring the right one when I was prepared for him.

Marriage was never part of my plans. I decided that I would not marry, because I did not want to have a failed marriage like my mother did. Thus, I always kept the guys at just a friendly distance. I knew that some of them, who were just friends, were interested; but I was too scared to let them know how fragile I really was. Perhaps I lost some good opportunities back then, but oh well …

Chapter 6

$$As\ Life\ Goes\ By$$

Between ages fifteen and seventeen, and then at the end of my nineteenth year, I was involved with a modelling group and even did extra work on Brazilian TV shows and catwalks. What a great time that was, a time of growth.

My modelling teacher was the best; I admired him so much. He told me much of what I know today: how to behave like a lady; how to sit, walk, and talk with elegance; how to have table manners; among other things. He saw in me someone I dreamed of becoming.

One day he said, "Jacky, you will go far in life."

He was right; here I am, in Australia, and could not be further away from home. But I joke.

When I was fifteen, my younger aunt—the one who is five years younger than me—and I went to visit her and my mother's sisters in Germany.

My aunt has always been one of my role models. She was an ex-model who was married to a German gentleman, and they lived a wealthy life. At the time, they had one child, and she was pregnant of her second. It was summertime in Europe, and this was my first overseas trip.

The adventure started just before we arrived. We noticed that some of the flight attendants, all of a sudden, were paying great attention to us. They closed down all the windows in broad daylight when we were just about to land.

When we got out, my aunt said, "My God, did you guys know that one of the turbines on your airplane was on fire?"

I must say I did not process that information until later that night, when I went to bed. This was one of my first encounters with death. Nonetheless, it was the best trip a poor teenaged girl could ever have. They took us everywhere, a trip within Europe by car; we even got lost in Zurich-Switzerland. How fancy … what a blessed adventure. I am grateful for them providing us with such an unforgettable trip.

Chapter 7

. . . .

Facing the Past

But you must be thinking, *What happened between my seventeenth and mid-nineteen years?*

Well, here comes my first love story—but let me explain what happened before that. After my infancy, my family never went back to the town in which I was born, the state where my father and uncle lived.

In April 1987 my stepfather's younger sister—a great friend who was about four years older than me—came over one weekend and asked if I would like to go back to where we were born, during June's school holidays, for four weeks. She wanted to get to know the town we both came from. We had no idea what it looked like since we both moved when very young. She heard there were amazing beaches and that it was a beautiful place, lively and full of culture.

You can just imagine that it took a lot of effort from us to convince my mother and her brother (my stepfather) to allow us to travel. Mum only permitted with the condition that although we could visit my dad, we were not allowed to stay at his house.

Back then I thought she was just jealous because she did not want me to be too close to Dad and his new wife, but today I know she had foreseen possibly losing me to that place. So we promised to return, and she gave her permission. We called my uncle to advise him of our arrival date, and also told my dad, as I wanted to meet my younger half siblings.

The bus tickets were purchased, and we saved as much money as possible to take on our little adventure. It was adventurous all right—we went from the southeast of Brazil to the northeast by bus. Back then it took three days and two nights, with so many stopovers during the course of the trip. But it was so much fun getting to see all those different states along the way.

Brazil is a huge and beautiful country. Each state is like a different country altogether—they have their own cuisines, dialects, music styles, dances, and folkloric clothing—it is an amazing place to explore. I felt like a tourist in my own home country, discovering the beauty in the diversity there. We were so excited.

It was a long and tiring trip, and on the third day we finally arrived at their bus terminal. My uncle—my dear angel from my childhood—was waiting for us. I was so happy to see him again, and although a little apprehensive, I felt blessed, curious to be back in the beautiful town in which I was born.

Everything was a new discovery; everything was different from where I came from, especially the food and the way they spoke—their accent was quite funny to me; they pronounced words like they were singing. I was delighted with the hot days and nights there and felt surprisingly at home. I love summertime, with the heat and the beaches. This is my kind of place, my tropical paradise. I love it!

I believe I was sent back there to start my self-therapy, my self-recovery from those sad and tragic episodes of my early life. In fact, I wasn't feeling bad about anything; on the contrary, it was exciting. I was falling in love with my hometown. That is how I always have faced life, with a positive attitude. Going back to my roots was my way to detach from a childhood trauma.

Dad came over to Uncle's home a week later to take us for a

lunch at his home; so I could meet my half brother and sisters. They lived quite comfortably in a large house and owned a few small businesses.

At first I was hesitant to go, although I was curious to meet the kids. Somehow, I felt like I was betraying my mother. Then, I decided to put that aside and thought: *Well, their issue is not mine. I will not take any sides.*

My cousin and I noticed that my father's new wife was nervous to meet me too. She had prepared a big feast, and the house was alive with all the other guests (her sisters and mother); they all instantly liked me and treated me as if I was always part of their family.

My cousin also felt at home, and our first uneasiness quickly vanished. Funny enough, I had the impression that I already knew her from somewhere. She was so sweet to me, treating me like her own daughter. As soon as I arrived there, she showed me my own bedroom, as they thought I had come to stay over for some days with them—wow, I had my own room in their house!— I never had one before; my brothers and I had shared a bunk bed in our room.

The best part of all was meeting my two little half sisters and brother, who were so cute. The boy, the middle child, quietly sat watching cartoons.

The younger girl looked exactly like the photo of my grandmother (Dad's mother). She was around two or three years old I believe, and she was so cute and cuddly.

The older one was fascinated and stayed by my side. Instantly she got so close to me and asked me to stay with them. That was tough to answer; my mother instantly came to my mind—we'd promised her to not stay at their house. I then replied that Dad should speak to my uncle, as we had no permission to sleep anywhere else.

Believing I got her off my case, she quickly turned to Dad and asked him to ask my uncle for his permission for us to stay at their place for the rest of our trip.

My cousin and I exchanged a scared and anxious look, and I thought, *Wow, now we're going to get into big trouble.*

My father thought this was a great and sensible idea, as my uncle's home was small and could not comfortably accommodate us for such a long holiday, especially because my uncle still had all his sons (four guys) living at home.

Dad thought it was better for everyone if we stayed at his place. Over there I would have a room to share with my cousin. Also, he had a car and could drive us to all the tourist places and the beaches.

This was a delicate situation. I knew my uncle would be concerned about my mother's orders and feelings—so was I—but Dad convinced my uncle, and he gave us permission to stay at Dad's.

We packet our bags, and off we went to stay the rest of our holiday in my father's new home.

Chapter 8

Love at First Sight

At first it felt awkward to be at my father's place, and I couldn't help but feel that I was somehow betraying Mum's trust and wishes. At the same time, my uncle agreed that it was best for us to stay at Dad's, and slowly I felt at home.

I got so much attention from my sister, the older one. When she was around ten or eleven, she would follow me wherever I went. Always stroking my hair, playing with my curls, saying she wished to be like me when she grew up. Dad and his wife were happy to have us there, and they made us feel comfortable and welcome.

They lived on a small dead-end street that was so alive. There were people of all ages everywhere, and Dad and my older half sister made sure to introduce us to everyone who passed by. They were proud to have us staying at their place.

At the end of their street was a volleyball game, with some players from other streets and suburbs who come over to compete every weekend in a friendly match.

They called it "the elite street" of that suburb. At the time, my father was the most well-known, successful, and respected person there, and his wife was much liked by all the neighbors. She was charismatic and had a kind and bubbly nature. Like my mother, she was a hard worker. I was fascinated to discover everything about them, and my initial bad feelings disappeared.

The Sunday was ending, and the sunset was beautiful; in spite of the tropical heat, there was a fresh breeze, and the sky was always so clear, full of stars. So different from where I came from. All the neighbors were sitting outside chatting, some lying on hammocks or sitting on rocking chairs; there were kids playing on the street, and the teenagers joined their friends to chat and play volleyball. I quickly fell in love with it all.

At this stage I had met a few girls who were living at the end of their street. One was a funny girl; everyone liked her. She made us laugh the whole time.

She told me I should meet this handsome guy who used to play volleyball there every weekend. He lived on another street not far from us. Just when she was finishing talking about the handsome guy, there he was, with a volleyball ball under his arm, walking toward the little grass court at the end of my father's street.

She was right, indeed —he was a hunk: tall, tanned, great figure, same age as me, and had the most beautiful and innocent smile I ever seen in a guy. I will call him Mr. K to protect his name. However, based on what my new friends mentioned, he was hotly contested by the girls over that suburb, and I did not think he would be interested in me, nor did I want to be involved with a womanizer.

But guess what? As soon as Mr. K saw me talking to her—who was his friend—he stopped to find out who the new girls on the block were. She introduced us, particularly me.

He said something like, "Wow, so should I stay away? Your father is a powerful guy here. I did not know he had such a beautiful daughter. Where were you hiding?"

Charming. I blushed, and notwithstanding the other girls who were there just to see him play, he asked, "Do you play volleyball?"

I shook my head.

He smiled and quickly replied, "I can teach you when I finish this game."

This time I nodded—I could not resist that smile. My cousin and all the other girls winked at each other and made fun of us.

Would he be the one to crash down the barriers ? All I knew was that when our eyes met for the first time, we knew something powerful happened, and although I was resisting it at first, for shyness or fear or rejection, I was certain as soon as I saw him that we would be together.

Do you believe in love at first sight? I sure do.

Chapter 9

"Don't Dream It's Over"

The volleyball match ended, and it started raining. We all got together in the garage of one of the girls who lived right in front of the courtyard and chatted all night long.

I was anxiously waiting for him to come over, but a bit disappointed that the rain would spoil my chances to get to know him better, with my pretense to learn how to play volleyball. To my surprise he came over with some friends from his team soon after the game ended, and we all stayed there laughing and carrying on as teenagers do. My trip was starting to get really interesting.

The rain eased up. Although we were all talking in a group, I felt that he wanted to talk to me alone, as Mr. K could not stop staring and smiling at me. So he asked me if I would like my first lesson.

We stayed there on the street, passing the ball to each other, and he took the opportunity to make an exciting interrogation, asking where I came from and how long I was staying, and even invited me to go out dancing in a nightclub near the beach on the following weekend. I happily accepted as the girls had organized a group of more than twenty of us to go together.

While we were talking, Dad came outside asking my cousin and me to get in as it was getting late. For some reason my father did not like Mr. K. My cousin and I, got inside and gossiped all night long about the great time we were having, the great people we'd met, and especially about Mr. K. She made fun of me, saying I fell in love with him at first sight. I denied it, of course. I could not believe it was happening to me.

During the following week, Dad took us everywhere. The beach was amazingly beautiful—I loved their way of living, was enjoying my holiday, loved to get to know my brother and sisters, to make new friends, and could not wait to see Mr. K again.

Because of middle-of-the-year school holidays, we all saw each other every day and night that week. The friendships grew stronger, and we soon had a large group meeting every night for chats, right in front of our mutual friends house.

My interest in Mr. K was growing fast; he was a handsome, funny, charming, witty, intelligent, and good soul with a white killer smile that took my breath away. That worried me, because I knew I would eventually have to return home.

The Saturday night finally arrived, and we all went to the nightclub. We danced the night away. He was a great dancer.

I noticed some girls hoping to be with him. So I kept to myself, having fun with my cousin and new friends.

In the 1980s in Brazilian nightclubs, there were always a time when the DJ played soft ballads for couples to dance to. I would run straight to the bathroom when those songs played to avoid unwanted guys asking me to dance. But not this time. The first song was "Don't Dream It's Over" by Crowded House.

I loved that song and was hoping he would ask me for a dance. I did not see him before the song started, so I decided to walk around the dance floor, just to see if he was already dancing with someone else.

When I returned from my first search, my friend said, "Jacky, stay here, because Mr. K wants to dance with you; he is going around the club looking for you, while you are going around looking for him." She knew how to be direct. I miss her.

Then I felt a hand on my shoulder, and there he was, asking me for a dance. "Don't Dream It's Over" became our song. How ironic destiny is. Crowded House is an Australian band, which I only found out once I met my Australian future ex-husband.

Well, this was our opportunity to be closer, and our first kiss happened. We stayed together for the rest of the night like a couple in love. He became my summer holiday boyfriend, and from that day on we could not be apart; we were indeed in love.

We saw each other every day and night. He took me to touristy places, and even to his house to meet his family. We got more attached the more time we spent together, and the thought of our separation at the end of the holiday season made us cry.

My father did not approve of our relationship because he thought my new boyfriend was not a good catch. Dad had other plans for me. My father used to go to places where high society people frequented. And these were the people he wanted me to get involved with. But we cannot plan those things—they just happen.

I had the best time of my life and will never forget how he made me feel so special. Unfortunately, it was the end of the holiday season, and I made a promise that I would come back. The plan was that I would finish that school year and return to live at my dad's home and finish high school there, just to be closer to him. We cried a lot when saying goodbye but with the hope to see each other at the end of the year.

Chapter 10

New Home, New Life

That was the hardest decision I'd had to make, because my mother always thought I was choosing my father over her. Little did she know the real reason I decided to move to my dad's place was because of my boyfriend—to be closer to him and live the pure love I was feeling. I thought I had found my soul mate, and I needed to give it a shot.

Naively, I did not realize I was breaking my poor mother's heart, because like every selfish teenager I was only thinking of myself. Today, I understand how much she got hurt with my decision and hope she has forgiven me for it.

There I went. I packed my bags and moved to my father's home at the beginning of the following year. I was so happy to see my boyfriend again; we were so much in love. Also, I was excited about my new life ahead—new home, new friends, new family, new high school, and new city.

I lived this sweet life for more than a year. Things were pretty good; I had great friends, a hot and loving boyfriend, great relationship with my stepmother and siblings, a great social life, and a job as a Catwalk trainer.

I was on my last year of high school, and Mr. K. and I even had plans to get married. But my relationship with my father was deteriorating. I discovered how he was treating my stepmother, and I did not like what I saw.

Dad and I had a big fight because he would not accept my boyfriend, and in the heat of the moment I accused him of trying to kill my mother—mind you, my half brother and sisters did not know anything about it until then—and this was sufficient for him to call Mum over and ask her to take me home, because I was disobeying and giving him trouble. I was not speaking to my father.

A week later Mum came to save me and took me back home. Once again Mr. K and I were pulled apart, but this time to never got back again. I remember the day I got on the bus, how much we both cried at the bus terminal.

I also remember my mother's words. Feeling sorry for me, she caressed my hair and said, "If this boy loves you, he will do anything to be near you, and then you'll know it's meant to be."

I cried myself to sleep, and then I had the longest and saddest trip back home.

Mr. K and I spoke all the time over the phone and wrote many letters to each other, but I did not see any effort on his part to come to me. He was scared and did not have the courage to leave his comfort zone, like I did. Although I still had feelings for him, time was a great friend, healing all wounds. I was disappointed in him and then started to think that my father might have had a higher vision of what was best for my life.

I decided then to move on and spread my wings, and this was when a trip to Japan came along. It was the best remedy for a broken heart—the beginning of a brand new world was waiting for me.

Chapter 11

. . . .

Living in Japan

After returning from my father's home, I decided to concentrate on my modelling career. Studying was no longer interesting, so I put that aside for a while. I did some catwalks and worked as an extra on a few TV shows. This helped me with my financial needs and put my failed love story behind me. Although I would never forget him, he was not only my first love, he was my first everything. The first one we never forget.

In the middle of 1989 a friend from modelling school had just come back from a trip in Japan, where she worked at a theme park, as part of their entertainment area. She was part of a Brazilian group of dancers. They stayed on a six-month contract and earned quite a reasonable monthly amount in American dollars, with everything about the whole trip paid for. I always said to my mother that one day I would leave and go abroad, and here came destiny presenting me with my first open door to my financial freedom. My aim was to earn enough to buy a bigger house for my mom. The five of us used to live in a tiny one-bedroom house. I knew the trip would not pay enough for a house but certainly would bring in a lot more than I have ever expected.

My friend asked me if I would like to be part of the next

group to leave Brazil to Japan in November that year. I jumped on the opportunity, and after passing the auditions, we left for Japan.

There we went, ten girls who became lifetime best friends. During the six months, so many things happened. We had so much fun after the shows, playing in the park like little kids, it was more fun than work. We would run away at night from the bosses to go to the city, laughing and carrying on with those crazy and funny Japanese friends we met. We were discovering a whole new culture, and although it clashed a lot with ours, it was not so unknown to us, as Brazil holds the largest number of Japanese immigrants.

I loved Japan and wished I could live there from the day we arrived; it felt like home. I truly believe I lived there in a past life. Learning the Japanese language was easy for me. Although being away from the family was hard, and four months after our arrival I end up in a Japanese hospital for a week because of a retroverted (tilted) uterus caused by physical stress.

For some of the girls, six months seemed to be a long time, but for me it went way too quickly. We were getting to the end of the contract when I made friends with a Japanese girl who invited me to come back so she could help me stay in the country, so I did.

We arrived back in Brazil at the beginning of May 1990, just a few weeks before I turned twenty-one. I had a big party to celebrate and invited all the girls.

My mother was so happy to see me back. The money I got for working helped us a lot. I bought a telephone line for her— back then, not everyone had one—and I replaced most of her furniture and gave her some money.

My mother was always my biggest supporter. She saw my trip as my opportunity to see the world, and to secure my financial life, but she never thought I would really fulfil my desire to live abroad. After being back from Japan for three months, I decided to return with one of the girls from my group, a dear friend. We both dreamed of staying there for a long period, perhaps to live.

Things did not really work out well for her, and she only stayed for a few months, but the adventurous and proud side of me did not want to lose sight of my dream to buy a house for my mother. I decided to stay longer.

One morning I woke up and discovered the crazy girl had left me with nothing in the fridge to eat but rice, milk, and instant noodles. I thought she just disappeared to her parents' house, because she was a rebellious and wealthy girl with unusual behaviors. But who am I to judge? Each to their own needs.

Nearly two weeks passed and she never returned. I had no money, just my return ticket, with no cash to even catch the Shinkansen (the Bullet Train) to the airport in Tokyo, as I was living in the countryside—more than two hours from the airport. My Japanese was not good enough to get me a job, and I had no food.

One rainy morning I was praying and crying, thinking, *What should I do?* I asked that while looking at the sky, and I said, "Is God in this part of the world?" I asked that because I saw them worshiping so many different gods.

Call it a miracle or divine providence, but at that exact moment the doorbell rang. I quickly wiped my tears, and through the peephole I saw a lady with a bag and a Bible in her hand. Then, I thought, *Oh dear Lord, there is a Jehovah's Witness here?* Remember, I had just asked if there was a God; I did not associate that divine intervention until later in life.

I opened the door and gestured to her, trying to say with my broken Japanese and sign language that I did not know how to speak Japanese. She looked at my puffy, crying eyes and bowed down to a bag on the floor and took out a little magazine. I thought, *Great, if I cannot speak, what makes her think I can read?*

Amazingly enough, she opened the magazine and pointed. The first phrase I saw was written in Portuguese: "You are not alone." I nearly fainted, and then started crying so much that at first she did not know what was happening. But she felt sorry for me and understood that something was wrong.

She then asked through gestures if she could come in. I let her in, and with my poor Japanese, I tried to explained what was happening. I'm not sure if she understood everything, but she quickly stood up, opened the cabinets and fridge, and saw that there was nothing to eat. I had been hungry for nearly two weeks, living on stale bread and expired milk.

She made a sign for me to wait, left her books there, and left with her purse. I did not understand a thing she said, but I got that she was going somewhere for help. After thirty minutes she came back with a few grocery shopping bags and filled up my fridge with food for the week.

This episode told me that God will always use whatever instrument he has at hand to reach out to us. Indeed, we are never alone. Today I think, *May God bless the daily house-approaching work of the Jehovah's Witnesses; my respect and eternal gratitude to them.*

I could not stop thanking God enough, and, of course, that lady too, for being at the right place at the right time. I told her that I needed to find a job to get some cash so I could pay the rent and survive until I had to go home. I asked if she could get me a job as a cleaner, because I was good at cleaning and would not need to speak Japanese.

She pondered for a while and said she would think of something. Then I remembered the crazy girl used to know an owner of a construction company not far from where I was living, and behind that construction company building were a few bedrooms for single guys from interstate who worked for them.

I asked her to help me convince the owner of that place to take me as their cleaner for the time being, to clean their rooms and the office for some cash. So she did, and he accepted me. I got paid good money, for it was hard work. Those guys were quite messy, and I cannot even mention here what I found under their beds.

They used to laugh at me, because in spite of my broken Japanese, I was always telling them off every time I cleaned their dirty rooms, and they found that cute. But I liked them; they were young, shy guys with little education but with big hearts and souls.

Weeks went by, and I was starting to get confident, standing on my two feet, growing fond of everyone and that beautiful country.

I never saw my guardian angel again (the Jehovah's Witness lady). I was working hard and making ends meet, but in the back of my mind, I was worried because my visa was about to expire, and I would have to leave Japan just when I was just starting to feel at home.

I made friends with the girl who was working at that construction company office. I told her that in Brazil I used to work in an accountancy company and that I was a fast typist. She then changed the keyboard to an English version and asked me to type some text in English. To her amazement I quickly completed the task. She realized I was an educated and smart young lady, and she told me I should not be working as a cleaner.

My experience there was another way life taught me to detach from conventions, from pride. When things get tough, I should make the best of what I had, of what life was presenting to me. I am grateful to Mum for being a strong and strict disciplinarian. She taught me at an early age to clean and cook, to have no fear or shame in making ends meet with honest hard work. That helped me when I most needed it.

By the second week I learned how to write and read Hiragana and Katakana, the two Japanese writing characters, and I learned it all in one day. All seemed easy and natural to me. My Japanese was improving fast, and within a month's time I could even hold up a conversation.

I do not recall the name of the girl from the office, but I

remember her being my second angel. She also used to work at night in a snack bar—her boss's cousins (an elderly couple) were the owners. It was a traditional, cozy, and small snack bar, highly frequented by some of the old rich people in that little city, and by the officers who used to work at the council centre.

They went there nearly every night after work to relax, chat, have some drinks and snacks, and to sing karaoke, a big Japanese passion. I am a firm believer that their soul gets cleansed and energized when they sing typical Japanese songs, like "Enka."

I stopped cleaning at the construction company, and the snack bar became my full time job. I started at 6:00 p.m. and finished at midnight. By the time we cleaned everything and got home, I was dead tired. I used to sleep until noon every day.

Prior to starting at the snack bar, I told my old boss that my visa was about to expire, and I was going to return home. But they were fond of me and wanted me to stay. He then asked me what he could do to help me obtain a visa. But due to his line of business, he could not sponsor me. Then he said I should marry a Japanese man to be able to stay. That idea did not please me at all at first (nothing against Japanese men, but I did not want to get married at twenty). Although I was sad to leave, I was thinking of returning home and had other plans for my life.

Then, all of a sudden, one of the guys whose room I used to clean was listening to our conversation and got into the discussion. He said, "I'll marry you, Jacky–san. That would help you but would also help me. I am just about to be transferred to another island as the foreman of a new project, and my family may soon push me into an arranged marriage, but I do not want that now. So if you marry me, I can fulfil my career aspiration and help you stay in the long run. I will come back here every time you need me."

Everyone on the room started to clap and celebrate, while I could not believe what I was hearing and how all had turned out. Right away I felt safe with his proposal, and we both got

moving toward our "wedding." Although I still scared that he would ask for something more, he never did. There he was, another angel that God had put on my path. We became good friends and got legally married the following week, and every six months after that he came back to visit.

He was my savior and a dear friend, a sweet and shy young man who had eliminated the possibility of finding love and getting married for some years—the time I was living in Japan as his wife. I respected him so much, as he has never asked me for anything more than my friendship. He seemed to be happy with his freedom and work life on the island he lived, so I guess everything worked out well for both of us.

One day, during one of his visits, I said I would be eternally grateful for what he had done for me, because due to my staying, I was able to help my family back home and save some money to buy them a nice home.

He never stopped surprising me and replied, "No, you do not have to be thankful. I am the one who should be thanking you, for giving me the opportunity to pay you back a favor from a past life. This is just payback time." Wow, that made me cry a lot, although back then I did not quite measure the profundity of his words. I did not understand what he meant about a past life. I am still so grateful, and although we have never seen or heard from each other since I left Japan, I always think highly of him and ask God to protect him wherever he may be.

I loved my life in Japan. Once I settled in, I attended school to clean up my grammar, to learn how to read, write, and perfect my Japanese. By the end of that year I was a fluent Japanese speaker. My bosses could not believe how fast I had learned and were amazed that although I was not of Japanese descent, I did not speak with a Brazilian accent. I was able to speak like a native and learned how to sing their songs the way they sang them. I love the Japanese culture and everything about it. I felt very much at home. Oh, I miss Japan!

My life there summarized in studying, working at the Snack

Bar, and also every now and then, singing with a Brazilian Bossa Nova band that I met during my second year. As I lived a quiet country life without much excitement, I had a lot of time on hand, so I used to ride my bike to a beautiful site to write poems. I've had a passion for writing since then.

One of the oldest Brazilian girls who came to Japan with me on that first group trip married a Japanese gentleman, and they lived in a nearby city. She was the only foreigner I knew there, and they became my family. I was at their house every Sunday morning and stayed over until Monday early afternoon. I loved them.

Her husband, although a fire fighter by trade, used to be a photographer for Canon cameras magazines, and I used to work for him in my spare time as a model. I liked those jobs, as they paid really well for such a short time. It was a shame they did not happen often.

I must say life was a bit lonely in Japan. I missed my family a lot, as I did not have many friends, besides the ones I mentioned plus a group of seniors who came to the snack bar nearly every night. But I understood that to get what I wanted, I would have to make some sacrifices, and the price I paid to be able to give my family a better life was being so far from them. I'm not sure whether I have learned the detachment lesson from these experience, because in the back of my mind, I always thought, *What if something happens with any of my family members and I am so far away?* I suffered with those thoughts, but I learned to deal with their absence in my daily life, in spite of dropping many quiet tears, because I missed home. What you focus on can be your strength.

It was not easy to live so far from home back in the 1980s and '90s. Remember, back then there was no Internet, mobile phones, etc. All communications were done through expensive and short telephone calls or handwritten letters. Luckily I was liked by those people, and they all treated me like a daughter. I loved them; they were my family for a long and lonely time.

Chapter 12

When Australia Meets Brazil in Japan

At the beginning of 1992, my life was about to change. After three years of not having a boyfriend, I was singing karaoke with a customer that night, at the snack bar where I worked. Two young and handsome Australian men came in. They were backpackers adventuring in Japan.

They were on their way to a city not far from where I was living, and from there they would be going back to Tokyo to continue their planned trip to Europe. However, synchronicity was working behind the scenes to make two different worlds come together in an unusual way. For some reason, their train stopped in the city I was living in, and they decided to explore that night.

Hungry from the trip, they found a noodle bar just beside the snack bar (coincidence?). At the Noodle Bar, they met one of the old ladies (another coincidence?) who used to come late at night to top off her drinks. In the midst of their conversation, the lady asked the two young Australian guys if they would like to meet an indigenous Brazilian girl from the Amazon. Guess who? Yes, me.

Much to their disappointment, they found a skinny, pale,

young Brazilian girl who was dressed in business attire and who looked nothing like an indigenous woman, much less like a Brazilian. I guess the lady liked them and wanted to keep their company, so to convince them to come for drinks with her. She sold them on a false ticket. Well, thank God she did that, otherwise I would not be here today.

Cutting a long love story short (as by itself would be another interesting book), that weird destiny brought me to meet my Australian ex-husband, the father of my son.

When he and his friend walked into the bar that night, my heart started pounding. After our marriage, I used to joke with him, saying that I did not fall for him at first sight—he did, though. I was actually interested in his friend at first, but he was too snobby, and my ex had such a caring and special way of looking at and talking to me that my attention quickly moved to him. He looked at me like he was seeing a precious doll.

Back then, I could hardly say hello in English. My boss got worried because no one could speak to them, to know what they wanted to drink. We lived in the countryside, and it was rare to see a foreigner. I was the only foreigner in that little town, besides a few occasional American exchange students.

My English went as far as, "How are you? My name is Jacky. The book is on the table." I must admit, I have come along way for someone who could not understand what he was saying and now is writing this book in English!

Lucky enough (here comes synchronicity again playing its part), one customer that night, who I had never seen before and who spoke fluent English, happily offered to sit at their table to help me serve them. I thought the guy just wanted an opportunity to practice his rusty English.

It was late at night and they ended up missing the train to the city they were aiming to catch before meeting the old lady, but they also got interested in staying over that night so they could visit some beautiful temples, which I offered to take them to see the following morning.

The ex asked me out to dinner, and how funny when he also invited that English-speaking Japanese gentleman, so he could be our translator. What an unusual sight—a Japanese man being the translator for an Australian and a Brazilian. Those things only seem to happen to me.

During dinner something odd happened. I noticed that at one stage the Japanese man said something to Mr. S. (let's refer to the ex like this), which cause him to have a doubtful face, but he said nothing in return.

Then, soon after, the man turned to me and said, "He wants to marry you."

I made a surprised face, but I said to him in Japanese, "Are you sure you can speak English? He just met me. How he could want to marry me?"

The guy just laughed in response. I laughed too, and Mr. S. laughed, not even knowing what was said.

When the man noticed that we were both directly communicating through gestures and drawings, he took a business card from his pocket, stood up, gave the card to Mr. S., and said in Japanese to me, "My job is done here. This is my card—when you guys get married, do not forget to send me an invitation. I always wanted to go to Australia."

I laughed, Mr. S. laughed once again, and we both thanked him. We stayed together trying to communicate through the universal language of love, and years after we both realized what that guy did.

We fell in love, but we both knew we were from different planets. Back then, he was an Australian backpacker on a working holiday visa, who was one and a half years younger than me, and who was just about to go to Europe to continue his adventurous trip. I was a "married" woman who had plans to stay in Japan for another year, so I could buy my mother a house, and after that, I had plans to move to Germany to live with my aunt. I did not want anything to spoil my plans, not even a romance. But who said you can fight destiny?

He ended up staying, and his friend went to Europe by himself, leaving him back in Japan, because of the indigenous Brazilian woman. I found a casual job for him and a place to live, and he occasionally taught English. We enjoyed a sweet romance, although things were not always rosy. The differences in culture, maturity, life experiences, languages, etc. were big roadblocks to overcome.

You might be asking what happened to my Japanese husband. Well, throughout all my time in Japan, he continued being part of my life. He came over every six months to visit and became a good friend to my ex and me. He knew that my time in Japan was about to end, and I guess it was good timing for him too, as he mentioned having met a lovely lady where he lived. So we got divorced.

Six month later Mr. S. asked me to marry him, and gave me an engagement ring. Although we loved each other, I did not feel we should get married at such a young age. I really had my doubts, as I wanted to achieve my goals first. Australia had never been on my mind before I met him. In fact, I knew nothing about Australia, besides the kangaroos and koalas and that it was essentially a big deserted island—at least that was what I thought then.

I was not sure if I wanted to live in a totally unknown country again, with no family. But like I said, life has its own peculiar ways of changing things.

Chapter 13

The Day I Met the Love of My Life: My Son

At the end of 1992 I discovered I was three months pregnant. That was a total surprise, especially because I was on the pill and was having my period as normal. This is a funny episode that I must tell you about.

Mr. S. and I had a fight, and I broke up with him about a week before I was continuously feeling ill. At first I though was a stomach bug of some sort. I was skinny, weighing less than 110 pounds, and ate like a sparrow. I also was having discomfort during sex with him, so I complained to my friend, who had just given birth to a beautiful baby girl a week earlier. I thought I had some kind of infection.

My friend got suspicious of my continuous sickness and subtly told me to see her doctor for a possible ovarian infection. When I got there, they asked me to do an urine test and made me wait. After twenty minutes, they asked me to take my clothes off, because the doctor would like to do an ultrasound.

I thought, *This is strange. Why would they want to do an ultrasound?* I had no clue. It even crossed my mind that I might have had a tumor.

Then, at some stage the doctor stopped at a spot on my

belly, turned the screen to me, pointed to a little blurry point that was pulsating, and said, "See this? This is one of the first organs to form—the heart."

I got that puzzled expression of someone who did not quite get what a person just said, and I replied, "What heart? Whose heart? Heart of what?"

The nurses then realized I did not know what was happening, and they started laughing and giggling.

The doctor turned to me and said in English, "Congratulations. You're going to be a mother. You are three months pregnant."

I started crying and said, "You must be wrong. It cannot be. I'm on the pill without fail and recently had my period as normal."

He then replied, "Oh, so you're on the pill? You know that the pill is only 99 percent effective, right ? Well, you're part of the 1 percent."

I got the biggest shock of my life. That was the last thing I thought I would hear on that day. No wonder I was feeling so sick. It was morning sickness.

A mix of emotions went through my mind, but anxiety and fear took over. I thought about a million things: How young I was to raise a kid, how all my plans would be gone now with that kind of responsibility, and that I would have to go back to Brazil and leave Japan, as well as my then boyfriend's reaction, etc.

The main thing I was worried about was what my mother would think of me. She always said, "Don't ever come here pregnant and without a father to look after your kid. I don't want you to be like those girls who have kids fathered by different men." I was terrified by that thought.

From the doctor, I went straight to my friend's house. I arrived there crying in desperation. "What should I do?"

She already knew I was pregnant, she just wanted me to discover for myself. My friend then said that although I had fought with my ex-boyfriend, he had the right to know that he

Eight years passed, and in the meanwhile, life went on. After many years apart, my ex and I became good friends and ended up getting back together.

Although we have grown a lot since our divorce, and at first it seemed that we had learned the necessary lessons to be happy the second time around, we grew in opposite directions. The relationship started well but once again did not work.

Today, I believe that the unresolved emotions of our original marriage, and of the past relationships we had since our divorce, were the instigators of our disagreements, thus turning what was so promising into a toxic relationship, because of old and polluted waters that passed under the bridge of our lives. Consequently, the differences between us took their place again.

I believe we got back together after so many years to finish what was left behind. Honestly, looking back now, it would never work. There was two opposite worlds trying to fit into each other, because it was "the devil we knew." I had grown a lot spiritually, and ironically, that also helped build a wall between us.

After three years together the second time around, we parted for the same reasons as we had in the first place. My love life was then declared dead.

Today, I question why life has allowed us to get together again, if we could never be what one expected from the other.

But there always will be a strong and unbreakable bond between us, the most beautiful and precious thing that life has given us, our son. This was one tough detachment lesson to overcome.

Earthly love is a complicated thing; I have never been sure what real love really is. Not even the poets are able to describe this pure feeling, for its essence is divine. We human beings are still so far from understanding. The love we know is based on physical sensations and emotions and on our own personal needs.

One thing I know for sure is what love is *not*—it is not love when there is dependency on reciprocity; it is not love when there is need of presence; it is not love when there is disrespect; it is not love when there is suffering; it is not love when you need to forgive; it is not love when there is fear of separation; it is not love when there is no trust; it is not love when there is control; it is not love when there is no complicity; it is not love when there is no freedom; it is not love when there is no loyalty; it is not love when there is no understanding; it is not love when there is no friendship; and it is not love when it does not last for eternity.

I see love today as the divine essence in all its universality, and if we live this essence in simplicity, we will then comprehend its profundity and transcend in it infinite qualities. Anything else is just a rehearsal!

Chapter 15

Small Fish in a Tank Full of Sharks

F ast forward to 2013, when I held a secure job as a manager of a prestigious corporate bank for seven years, and looking back, I do not even know how I got there. Prior to that I was just about to get terminated from a local bank because they were relocating my whole department to their head office, in another state.

Unexpectedly but at the exact needed moment (here comes synchronicity again), I received a phone call from the head of operations of this bank, offering me the same position I had applied for three years earlier. At first, I thought it was a Godsend, as it saved me from unemployment, but that job was the most challenging experience I ever had in my professional life. It has put me through difficult situations, pushing me in all directions.

I was pushed beyond my professional capacities—as when I joined the bank, I did not have the required skills to lead the two distinct teams I was managing. Pushed beyond my self-pride—due to experiencing unfair treatments, which has played on my self-esteem. Pushed beyond my self-worth—as I did not have the courage to leave, in spite of it all, because I had lost my self-confidence, and the industry I was working for had just collapsed due to the world's financial crisis. To top it off, I got way too comfortable with my pay, which used to cover my financial commitments and small luxuries.

We can say that I sold my soul to the devil for material and illusionary needs, and for a status quo that, in fact, did not exist, as over time I ended up being just part of the furniture, that go-to person who had a lot of technical skills but never had the chance to move up the career ladder because I refused to be part of the political games.

I believe the main reasons were because I showed no fear and was bold with my points of view in regard to the inconsistency of fairness. Also, I was way too honest for the likes of some big egos that saw me as threat because I made no efforts to inflate their ego. That certainly did not help me, so I was never made a part of their closed team.

The truth is, I was like a fish out of water in a tank full of sharks. I was too much of a humanitarian and not a good fit in the corporate environment. In the end I was just making ends meet. Every day it was depressing for me to face those people (except for my staff, who were like a family).

I knew deep down that I was a waste in that kind of toxic environment. I had so much to give, and that was not the right place to do it. My professional dissatisfaction was indirectly affecting all areas of my life. I felt trapped, and things were not so wonderful in my love, health, and spiritual sectors.

Every day I watched the faces of those executives on the train of life, and I saw a lack of brightness and lack of authentic joy. They wore their corporate personas and status quos to compete for success in search of professional recognition, and to achieve financial security.

Along the way, although they may reached their goals, the vast majority also conquered the top of the emotional stress ladder, achieving an existential emptiness, consequently spending their hard-earned money on psychiatrists dealing with depression and burnout.

Many greatly reduced their human capacity to recognize their own distance from loved ones. They could no longer notice the beauty in the little things around them and what really matters in life. With a blind eye to the fragility of those in need of their attention, they paid a high price for their dull pride, for living in an egotistic world of illusory superficiality, where, most of the time, the smartest subjugates what they consider the weakest.

I often analyzed what this constant pursuit of self-victory was saying. What are they hiding from, where is their true self, why are they so lost on materiality? It is not a crime to go after success as long as you do not lose yourself in it, forgetting those who helped you get there.

This is lack of humanization within the corporate world's action plans. But I believe it will eventually implode if they do not harmonize those plans with the whole, by being mindful of what their decisions may trigger on their subordinates' lives. A creation of a healthy interaction and balance between being and having is an underlined silent call. They, the so-called superiors, should not forget that the blood that runs in its veins, and the brains that provide their successful ideas, are still of humans.

Chapter 16

Health Issues

I have suffered for years with my womanhood area (uterus). That time of the month was hell for me. Once I heard, "This is a woman's healthy area," but for me was the contrary, my monthly sickness. And the stress I went through did not help. I believe I somatized the work and love frustrations into this areas, creating two huge fibroses, which had compromised my uterus, resulting in a hysterectomy.

Today I know that if we deviate from our true path, our internal systems come to a halt. Our true path is our calling in life; the one that makes us feel as if we were serving a purpose no matter how big or small it may be. And if we stray from that, our spirit (through the mind), releases electrical charges from our subconscious to the physical body, as an alert that something in our being is going against its true nature. If the calling goes unheard, those electrical currents will eventually accumulate itself, and affect a part of the body that it is mostly related to our emotions.

Let's think for example in my case. To me, the uterus represents the birth of life, motherhood, security, mother and father, childhood, my own sexual experiences and desires; all parts of my life that I have faced difficulties, distress, or some kind of pain. I believe that, the majority of sickness are psychosomatic.

I remember the day when my doctor said, "Yes, Jacky, we will have to remove your uterus. When would you like to do that? If you choose to go to a public hospital, it will take three to six months on a waiting list, but if you want to go through your private health coverage, I am available at such-and-such hospitals as early as next week."

She went on, giving me a booklet showing three different ways to perform the surgery, paying little attention to my shocked expression. I posed only one question: "Doctor, would you please tell me if these problems affected my sexual desire?"

She bluntly answered, "Oh, dear, I would be surprised if you have any sex drive at all."

I left the doctor's office that afternoon totally distressed. Walking toward my car, I did not see anything around me. I don't know how I got there as I had so many thoughts running through my head at that time. It did not take long for the tears to fall copiously, and when I got into my car, I stayed there for thirty minutes, looking at the exam results and crying with my heart and soul.

To be honest, I did not even know why I was crying with so much pain. I just felt so lonely, and millions of thoughts came to mind. *Oh dear Lord, I am still young enough, and If I can not be a mother again, that would close some doors of love. I have only one son. What if I fall in love with someone who wishes to have a child with me? I would be unable to do so." (PS—not that I wanted to, but this was what I thought—crazy, I know!)*

Then my ex-husband came into my mind. I now had the explanation for some disappointments between us. I felt like calling him just to say, "I'm so sorry, I hope you can understand." Oh never mind!

Feeling quite lost, I went home to think about my surgery choices and got instantly depressed. With no family in Australia, I desperately needed a shoulder to cry on. I needed Mum's lap to curl up on and weep like a hurt child. Thank God for friends— the family we choose. One of them, my special earthly angel in this country, came to my aid. I had no idea that this type of surgery could trigger a pre- and post-depressive state of mind.

I recalled that the last time I was in a hospital was for my caesarean, when my son came into this world. When discussing my options with my friend, I realized I could not wait any longer to have this procedure done; this was taking the life out of me. For many years I suffered with it and had procrastinated, as I always do when the matter is linked to health. I am one of those people who only goes to a doctor when things are pretty bad.

However, this time I could no longer postpone it as it was affecting my work life too. I had no energy to wake up early in the morning, getting out of bed was a drag, and the work did not motivate me. I was always late.

When I found out about the costs, I was determined to have it done as soon as possible, but when I heard that the health insurance would only cover a portion of it, leaving me with a great amount to pay out of pocket, and I had no money to put toward it, what could I do?

I called my mother and also spoke to my sister-in-law in Brazil, who I knew worked for the government, and she was the main person to help me make the decision to go back home and do it over there. Also, I thought that being close to and cared for by my mother and family would be the ideal support I needed so much.

That was not enough to shake things around, and another surprise came along. Just a week before my departure to Brazil for the surgery, my boss calls me into a meeting with the HR manager and advised me that my position would be made redundant once I was back.

Looking at his face, I just wanted a hole to appear for me to fall into and disappear. That shook me—oh yes it did. I was just about to take three months off for a surgery, a lifetime postponed decision, and then would be coming back to no job and lots of debt.

My health came first in the end, and as soon as I focused

on that, everything else lost its meaning. Unable to emotionally and mentally stay at work, I went home early on that day.

There was a mix of emotions: anger, frustration, and fear, and on the train ride back to my apartment, I looked at the sky and asked, "Okay, God, please tell me what you want from me."

I heard a subtle but clear voice saying, "Detachment—the lesson is detachment."

In a moment of lucidity, after a deep and long breath, I understood that something was propelling all those events to happen, for a much higher purpose. Something was pushing me toward my self-awakening journey.

Well, those profound thoughts did not last long, and the "poor me" mind set came to play its part. I cried myself to sleep that night.

The pressure was getting to me, and going back to work for the rest of the week was tough. I no longer felt like part of the furniture, and every single time I stepped into the office it was making me physically ill. I could not wait to get away from it.

Chapter 17

The Surgery

The day to go to Brazil had arrived. I knew I was taking a shot in the dark, as I was leaving for unknown possibilities, not certain that I would be able to have the surgery done, as they had different medical practices, but I needed to try. However, God had a special card up his sleeve. I just needed to do my part and trust in it.

The universe put another angel on my path. Someone who has become a special friend. She worked for the best public hospital in the city where my mother lives. With her help and the help of my sister-in-law, who was actually the person to convince me to go to Brazil for this surgery, a month after I arrived I had everything worked out, and with the best doctors in town.

I felt so blessed with their support. This special girl was holding my hand in the surgery room, because I was shaking like a leaf in a storm, nervous and scared. I know she does not like me to call her that, but she was my earthly angel, an instrument of God, when I most needed one, and for this I will be eternally grateful. Thank you, my dear friend and sister-in-law.

I must say the Brazilian doctors were reluctant to go through with it. Even though the exams from Australia showed that I needed this operation, they advised me they were only going to perform this procedure on me because they knew I had come from overseas to do it, and that due to my work commitments, I could not stay in Brazil any longer.

But if I was living there, they would first put me on a specific medicine for one year, to see if the myomas (fibroids) and period fluctuations would reduce their size and the pain would ease, prior to making the final decision to proceed with such an invasive operation as a hysterectomy. Especially because of my age. I knew then that I was in great and responsible hands … I understood why I was propelled to go back home for this.

However, the doctors had put the decision to go through with it or not in my hands. I took a week to think about it. I drew my courage from the two most important and strong woman in my life, my mother and grandmother, as well as an old friend who subtly gave me the piece of advice to have courage and trust in God. They told me to get rid of the suffering once and for all, and to not fear, as God and the angels would be with me.

After nearly a couple of months of various pre-operation exams, my mother and I returned to my doctor's appointment on a Friday afternoon, to advise him that I had decided to go ahead with it. To my and the doctors' surprise, something funny happened, which confirmed my decision. My mother was casually telling the doctor how relieved she was feeling with my decision, as her own paternal grandmother and my paternal grandmother both died from uterine cancer.

The doctor looked at me with a perplexed expression and said, "Why didn't you ever tell me that?"

I turned to my mother and said, "Why didn't you ever tell me that, Mum ?"

We both looked at each other. Mom said that she didn't think it was important.

The doctor and I both understood then that there was a higher reason for my being there. He quickly opened his calendar and said, "Okay, Jacqueline, I'm available on next Tuesday—should we do it then?"

What a relief—I must have some merits with the Creator, or someone up there really loves me, because all had fallen into place at the exact right time. The day of the surgery arrived, and I was shaking so much. I had my friend holding my hands in the operation room, until I was put to sleep. Being in Brazil with my family during that time was essential for the success of my full recovery.

My mother and middle brother dedicated their time to look after me as was in so much pain. Now, I can say that this was the best decision I had ever made to my personal life. I have never looked back—only to recognize that this was another lesson of detachment.

After three months of going through a lot of pain, being spoiled, and seventeen pounds heavier, I was ready to return to Australia to face my redundancy. Leaving home was hard. I could never thank my mother, brother, sister–in-law, and dear friends enough. I am eternally grateful for their love, kindness, and patience.

Chapter 18

Redundancy

Agreements were made to get a payout and be gone. The way all it was done, from the beginning, I knew it was unfair and thought of fighting for it, as I had kept journals of the unfair treatments I had received in that company over the years. But I decided to take my third step toward detachment and leave with dignity, not causing any commotions. I thought, in life we must choose our battles, and this one was not worth it.

Remember, I was just a small fish in that big tank full of sharks. Everything was propelling me to move from where I was and face the challenges that would come with those changes, in order to eliminate from my life once and for all, what no longer served a purpose. I chose to look at the positive side of things and read between the lines of what the universe was trying to tell me.

When life is pushing and forcing you to make the decision that you are postponing, do not run away anymore. Everything happens for our improvement, and fear may be preventing you to take the course of actions that most will favor you in the long term. Lessons learned.

Today, I thank my bosses for having maneuvered me out; this was the only good thing they had ever done for me, as I probably would still be there, unhappy and complaining, but with no courage to do something about it.

That was indeed a blessing in disguise. A toxic environment can affect your physical and emotional health.

A window of my life was closing because I needed to be able to see the open doors ahead, and fighting against it would just have held me back, hindering my new path and opportunities.

What I learned from all that was how the universe works; if you are not responding to its call, something big comes to switch things around in an unexpected and harsh way; and the hidden lessons of suffering is being able to see it all without fear, and as a surmountable challenge. We only suffer with those changes when we keep holding onto the past, in fear of an unknown future. Remember, when everything feels like the end, it is actually just the beginning of a new direction.

At the end of that month I received the funds from my termination package, and it was just enough for me to pay some debts and take a little time to find another job, as I was too scared about what had happened, and was on the edge of depression. Back then, I even considered the possibility of returning to my home country, after twenty-five years of living abroad. That did not last long, as every time I thought about this possibility, I got an internal uneasiness saying, *It's not time yet.*

We must read those signs, what we call gut feelings. Through my process of internalization, I learned how to pay attention to them and understand that gut feelings are, in fact, our higher-self imprinting its own truth through the sensations of our physical body. If we notice it and endeavor to obey this inner voice, it will guide us in the right direction. This is the reason so many masters teach us to seek the answers within.

Pay attention to how certain situations in your life make you feel, and which physical and emotional reaction is linked to that specific situation, person, thought, etc. For the less intuitive ones, the answers of what is good or bad for you can be found in your physical sensations—how it makes your body feel. Pay attention!

Chapter 19

The Spiritual Sector of My Life

I have always been a spiritual person. I like to have an open mind, to read and learn from different types of sources of divinity. But although I was raised to call myself as Catholic, I never resonated with it and did not like the idea of being attached to one specific type of faith or doctrine. Deep down, I knew God was everywhere, mostly within.

My mother was never really inclined toward religion, although she has profound faith in God, Jesus, and Mother Mary. My grandmother took me to Mass in my early childhood and convinced my mother to enroll me for my first communion.

The day before my first communion, something really funny happened. I had to confess my sins to the priest. Now, you can imagine a shy and quiet seven-year-old girl looking at the man who was asking me all those questions, questions that made no sense to me. I was so scared of him and God, his God, of course, as I could not think of any sin I had committed until that day.

I could not get out of there without confessing. I had to say something. If up to that day I had not committed any sin, I was just about to commit my first one—I lied to the priest. I made up a story that I had pulled my aunt's hair and I was really sorry because it hurt her a lot.

He smiled and prescribed two Our Fathers and two Hail Mary prayers. Then I was acquitted and blessed by him, and off I went feeling so relieved. I never told that to anyone; I was too ashamed, but now I am publicly confessing my first and most naïve sin.

My mother was raised as a Catholic, but she never actually practiced it; not did she impose anything onto us. When we were kids, my middle brother and I went to a children's afternoon Sunday school class at a Presbyterian church at the end of our street.

The main reasons I went there was because they sang, told us Bible stories in the form of fairy tales, organized street games with us, and best of all, provided delicious snacks at the end. I am quite sure that the snacks were used to keep us there until the end and to keep us coming back every Sunday. Back then we were quite poor, and my mother, a single mom struggling to make ends meet, did not have spare money to take us out. So we couldn't wait for Sunday's church, it was so much fun, and although it was a different religion from hers, she actually liked it and felt relieved when we were there. It was a safe place that kept us out of mischief.

My two brothers and I went different ways in regard to spiritual beliefs, but that never was an issue between us, as we respected each others' paths. I believe there is a piece of the truth in every religious belief, but each one of us is an individual and on a unique road of spiritual enlightenment in accordance with our own psychological, moral, and intellectual development.

We are exactly where our affinity and level of comprehension of God has taken us. Thus, all religions are necessary, because each of us are on different levels of soul evolution. I believe that all paths will lead you to the Almighty; as long as the path you choose is in accordance to the law of divine love.

I have experienced good examples of this statement throughout my life, as I had a few encounters with different religions: first my Catholic background and then the Presbyterian church in my childhood. During my adolescence and while living in Japan, I heard a knock on my door, and to my surprise, a Jehovah's Witness lady saved me (see chapter 11).

Then, here in Australia, prior to my marriage break-up, after another prayer, two young Mormon gentlemen knocked on my door to deliver the exact words I needed at that time.

The key point is that throughout my years, God has come through every messenger available, every Light Worker from many different ways, beliefs, and times. Therefore, I understand that he/she/it, whatever you want to call it, is in all of them, using that type of resource to reconnect you to the Source, to itself.

I believe the truth is within each of us. We can be taught concepts about it, but not the truth itself. The true spiritual path is the one to leads us to discover the essence of our own being. Our truth is reflected in our life choices, in the way we think, act, react, and love. It is stored in mental and spiritual files of our subconscious and in the soul, which occasionally comes up as intuitive divine wisdom. Thus, any point of view that puts a full stop on spirituality becomes dogmatic.

Remembering all those close encounters with God, I noticed how blessed I have been all my life. There was always a helping hand sent from above, showing me direction. Also, it suggests that we must respect the work and spiritual path of each other, as one may end up being your earthly angel. Those people had no idea they were an instrument of the infinite love sent to me.

One thing is for sure: our mother's simple and beautiful faith in God's powers was so strong and so infectious that we had no other choice but to go with it.

Soon after my divorce, I was introduced to the spiritist doctrine through a great friend of mine, another earthly angel. "Spiritism is a lesson of love and everlasting life, in a continued pursuit of self-improvement, and harmony with all the creation throughout multiple existences. It reveals new and more profound concepts with respect to God, the universe, mankind, the spirits and the laws which govern life. Even more, it reveals what we are, from where we have originated, to where we shall go, and the cause of our pains and sufferings. Spiritism touches on all areas of human knowledge, of all activities and the behavior of Human Beings."

This was then my calling and spiritual finding. Today I believe that my friend was put on my path directed by my own personal spiritual guides to help me acquire a solid knowledge base of spirituality, which the doctrine so beautifully offers.

I remember the day she gave me *The Spirits' Book* by Allan Kardec (first published in 1857). This is one of the main doctrine book of Spiritism. It addresses questions and answers from spirits of a higher order. They spoke about life, life's purpose, the life after life, and everything in it. It was the most logical, philosophical, and scientific information that I came across at the time. And its religious aspect stems from the moral teachings and examples of Jesus Christ. I always had those questions in the back of my mind but could never find such clear answers in one place.

The book came as a light in the shadow in which I was living. I couldn't get enough; it answered my questions in a deep and profound way, but at the same time in a logical manner. I had the impression that I had read that book before. I had so many déjà vu experiences while reading it that I had the feeling I knew all the answers. I thought, *This is exactly what I think about all this,* but did not know how to put it into words.

To my surprise, when relating this feeling to my friend, she said, "I am not surprised at all, Jacky, since, in fact, you have already read this book, my dear. You have been prepared before this lifetime to pass on all those pieces of information to the English speaking people of this country. This is the main reason the universe brought you here."

I knew she was a sensitive and inspired person, but back then, I thought, *Oh dear Lord, she's crazy.* Time proved me wrong, and my friend was partially right.

In fact, I was the one who end up as the person dedicating more than ten years of my life to disseminating those words within a spiritist institution where I became a spiritual facilitator and a vice president of their charity foundation. This place was my spiritual bread and water, my resource of peace and where I got my strength when other parts of my life were falling apart.

I loved every bit of it: the people, my volunteer work, the knowledge I was so rapidly absorbing, the atmosphere, the spiritual teachers and guides. I used to wish and dream that one day this would become my only and real job.

I found myself when giving myself to others. I believe that was the purpose of my life, and at the time I thought it was the only way I could do it. What pleased me was that I never saw Spiritism as a religion; I always said, "For those who deeply study and understand its codifier, and have no atavism from previous religions. Spiritism is, in fact, a life philosophy."

However, like my mother says, "Where there are humans, there always will be ego issues."

Unfortunately, after all these years, everything went sour. Although we were trying our best, our pride got in the way of a long companionship. The sad thing is to realize that all profound preaching can lose its reasons and meaning, when in practice it is submitted by contradictory actions. I was then pushed to give up all my responsibilities, since I no longer felt at home.

Nonetheless, I will be eternally thankful for the opportunities I had, and will always hold close to my heart all of those people that were part of my spiritual journey in this life time. The spiritist doctrine gave me a solid base for my spiritual knowledge.

Leaving this institution broke my heart, even more than my second failed attempt to marriage, as that place was my sanctuary where I could recharge my soul batteries and where I felt protected. But I believe that God has set out a map guide to each soul, and every single one must follow his or her own path in order to end up at the same source—the events of my life were proving that to me.

This was another tough lesson of detachment. Perhaps the toughest, I thought then, because in order for us to have a happy and stable life, our main four pillars of strength must be in balance: our health, our financial life, our relationships, and our spirituality.

None of those areas of my life was in good shape, which consequently led me to the bane of the century, depression.

Chapter 20

· ·

The Dark Night of the Soul

Back at home, the months passed in monotony and darkness, where I saw myself sinking in the quicksand of depression. I had no wish to pursue other spiritual centers. To top it off, I'd gained more than fifteen pounds because of the operation, shaking my self-esteem. I used to wake up feeling heavy and tired.

I looked at myself in the mirror and noticed that my matted hair and changing body and face were showing signs of carelessness and age. The days outside were beautiful, and there I was, inside my apartment with no desire to get out, not even to take the garbage to the cans outside. Summer went and autumn came quickly, and I was lost in reverie and self-pity. But deep down I enjoyed the emptiness of time.

For some unknown reason I was happy to be dragged into loneliness, inside my little world, taking short steps out, learning more about the real me, the person I discovered within the dark night of the soul. In spite of it all, each morning I thanked God for one more day of life, and this was part of my morning routine. At this point I started talking to my guardian angel. "Hey you, loving sister, I know you can hear me, but I still do not know where to go, so please shed some light."

Lost in those thoughts, I felt compelled to write.

Active Spectator

Time passes slowly through the window of my eyes. Observing life outside, crossing the streets, everything seems to run rampant in synchronicity and composure.

Hence, I see the avenues, the cars, people who come and go in complicity … in the illusion of an urban life.

I wish I could play that dusty guitar, forgotten and pushed against the wall of my room, to sustain these reflections, in an old rhyme song.

I wish I could go back in time, to revise my steps, walking against the wind, dreaming of a promising future, to make the old ways better, and the new ways with a better old.

Through these windows nothing changes; life does not wait, I try to understand … it follows, always beautifully and safely for those who know how to live …

From social media, everything changes; the smiles in photos seem to sell appearances in a world of madness, a mere illusion of a wishing well.

I understand that life calls in for good communication, and to make sense amid farewells, to learn from pain and to smile with the new generation.

In this world alone, lost in reverie, I take refuge in the shelter of my home, walking through the lines of those thoughts … I am an active spectator in a world that seems to run, with steps on hold.

Every day I would write, read, and post messages of inspirations on social media, to soothe my soul in the hope that it could touch the hearts of those that would identify themselves with my moments of loneliness. Although, besides my mother and brother, they really had no clue what I was going through. But doing this gave me feelings of worthiness, and my days went by faster. Sometimes, I listened to music in the hope of lifting my mood.

On one of these occasions, an old song started playing,

bringing memories of my adolescent years, and a phrase of the song stood out: "What are you going to be when you grow up? Every day here looks like Sunday, but remember it is Monday, and you have nothing to show." Those words felt like arrows into my conscience, but enough reason to get me inspired.

Then I wrote:

Routine

In this empty routine we follow our script, with no time to look to the side. We walk the same steps in search of livelihood. Lamenting about the same choirs, the monotony of the everyday life.

We cry the same tears but do nothing to get out of this disillusionment. We are afraid to act differently and lose the thread of life. Aspiring to the same desires without the courage to find the exit. Apologizing for the same lies, because it is better than nothing.

We are driven by the same mass who disagrees with our soul wishes. We project our dreams onto the children yet to come, transferring the same ideas inherited from family.

We suffocate their free wings in their self-searching, forgetting that they have their right to freedom of thought. We learn to live with it, this crushing routine, appreciating what we have while remaining in the same disdain.

We face our reality, because this is what God wanted. It is easy to blame divinity for our lack of courage. Then, conformity masquerades our own dissatisfactions, helping us to survive until the end of the day.

Chapter 21

Feeling Guilt Is a Big No-No

Among all those reflections and self-searching, my self-esteem was in bad shape. In spite of all my attempts and qualifications, I had no luck in getting calls for a job interview. At the time, deep within, I had no desire to go back to that corporate world and office environment.

I was scarred for life, so I felt, but every time I looked at my bank account to pay bills, the money was disappearing, and nothing was changing. The bills echoed in my conscience like earthbound spirits who do not leave you alone until you pay attention to them.

Feeling guilty was not helping. Guilt is the worst enemy of true happiness and self-esteem. It is indeed the worst thing you can ever do to your soul.

Society and religions, within their doctrines of "right or wrong," created and cultivated in us certain ideas on how we should judge ourselves for every situation in our lives. Guilt is the most lethal weapon against a clear conscience and peace of mind. It keeps us in a web, under the control of those who see us as easy prey for their manipulation. It blocks our ability to make the right decisions and to believe that we deserve forgiveness.

I used to tell myself every day, "Jacky, free yourself from

any guilt, as there is only a right or wrong within what your conscience suggests." Today I see that everything I have done was the best I could do with the vision and knowledge I held at that time of my life. Forgiving and loving ourselves is a must, so we may see in other beings that are able to rebuild themselves by accepting their own faults. This was a normal daily conversation with me, myself, and I. It was my personal version of self-soul therapy.

When we learn to be at peace with our own conscience by accepting our weaknesses, we are also more susceptible to a nonjudgmental love. It does not mean we will no longer have consciousness of our wrongdoings, but we can certainly look at them as learning paths that promote our transformation to our better selves.

Traditional religions were the greater contributor of feeding guilt into society, but we must eliminate it from our mind and soul in order to create a life full of happy possibilities. Theoretically, I knew all that, but it is easier said than done.

Nonetheless, when you start to look within, as a being in the process of self-reparation, all wrongdoings just become your roadmap for today and tomorrow's better you. Be kind to the yesterday version of you—that person did not know better.

Chapter 22

When Your Son Becomes Your Father

My emotions were like a roller coaster, but there were days that I was more cheerful; those were the days I was writing those messages, as it kept me occupied.

On a low day, my son came home from work and looked at me with sadness, as he did not recognize that woman lying on the couch in the dark. She did not resemble the strong and secure mother, wife, spiritual teacher, and executive that I once was. I lay on that couch for the whole afternoon, the room in pitch black darkness, the only light coming from my laptop screen with an open social media window—my only open window to the world outside.

I used to stay like this for hours and days, in deep thoughts, analyzing where I went wrong, how I could get out of it, and trying to understand the deep meaning of the word detachment, as it kept coming back to hunt me.

Then, on that night, a short but special dialogue happened between us:

Son: What's going on Mom, something wrong? I've never seen you like this.

Me: Yes, something's wrong but I don't know what.

Son: I can see in your eyes and your ways—what are you thinking?

Me: My life, son—I'm thinking about my life. I don't know what to do. I am lost.

Son: Do what your heart is telling you. Do not do what the mind is saying. Listen to me, Mom; listen to your heart, not your mind.

He then left the room, and uncertainties became certainties. I sat before the image of a wise and old soul right in front of me, and he was my son, who, in his early twenties, was giving me pieces of advice, showing me the way out of that depressive state of mind. He was advocating to inspire my soul reflections, and as I could not hold them in any longer, tears once again fell silently.

I do not believe he understood how deeply his words touched me. I doubt he even remembers this. From that day on our relationship became stronger and deeper; we both saw each other with different eyes. There was a telepathic thing going on between us; we could feel when one was thinking about the other.

I read somewhere that telepathy occurs when the thinking mind sends waves of fluids that vibrates in the desired direction, shaping image of the message in the mind of the receiver. That made so much sense to me.

I love this beautiful soul who gave me the privilege to be his mother in this lifetime.

Chapter 23

Retrospective

When we have no perspectives and are feeling lost, the first thing we tend to do is a self-analysis and retrospective of our life. Coming to that time in life when uncertainties take place, we become unsure if the path we followed satisfied its purpose, or if dissatisfaction comes from what we missed trying.

I was facing a time when I was unsure if the decisions I made were correct, or if I had succeeded more out of those times I had made mistakes. That time and age where we look at the past as a great teacher but are not sure if we were great learners (would that be what they call a midlife crisis?). The time when what we thought was happiness was actually proved not to be capable of holding its meaning over the years. The time in life when we learn to see beauty in simple things, as if we are looking at them for the first time, when we think we are resolved with what we have and are, only to find that we have much more than we need and became much less than we should have. The time a whirlwind of emotions arose from nothing, as if nothingness would be able to hide the truth within. When we realize that we went so far to find exactly what was already so close. When the age spots we see in the mirror represent the farewells of our vital fluids, knowing that age is actually in the mind.

That time when you see that the clock of life will not stop with your sorrows, because if did, we would be the viewers of its end. When we recognize that humility, wisdom, and selflessness are values of a few and without them we have paid a high price. That time when we know that the joy of living is going through today with the best of us, with no fear of tomorrow. Well, I am holding the hope that the best is yet to come.

Chapter 24

The Voice

One morning, going through my coffee-making sanctuary routine (something I treasured and missed), I heard a voice saying, "Pick up the paper and write; once you write, spread those words to the world. Read them carefully, as they are all firstly written for you, but your gift will be able to reach many afar."

I did not question that, nor did I think I was going crazy, for craziness is the lack of creativity and freedom of thoughts. What is normality in a world like ours, right?

So, from that day on, the writing increased. At first, they came as verses and poems, and then they started to form messages to inspire my soul reflections. Everything was a reason to write; if I heard a word such as courage, the phrases poured into my head, with full strokes and in such speed that I could not stop thinking about what was being said. Every single time I read them, I got surprised.

Then another earthly angel, a dear friend and spiritual son who also writes verses and poems, read my writings and said, "Jacky, for a person who does not have any technical knowledge of writing, this is quite good. Make a blog and post them there, so they can be saved online."

I heard him and made my own blog, named Inspire Soul

Reflections; I understood that the universe was showing me through this beautiful soul the way I could reach people afar.

After months of depression, my writings were acting as my "spiritual Prozac"; they were the remedy I needed to get out of that state of mind. Every day I wrote five or more texts and spread them through social media and on my blog. I had decided to write in both languages (Portuguese and English) so I could reach even more people from my both worlds.

It was rewarding to receive feedback from people I never saw in my life, saying, "Thank you, I needed to read that today. It is like you wrote for me," and "Thank you for being a vessel of light."

Then, another friend came to me and said, "Jacky, do you realize that your writings have been seen by more than twenty thousand people over the Internet? I myself read them when I am feeling down."

I really had no idea. I had not stopped to pay attention to this, nor could imagine that she was reading them. Her words made me feel so alive and gave me that special sensation we get when we are at service with someone in need. In fact, little did they know that I was actually writing them for my own sanity. That gave me the inspiration and insight that I was on the right track to escaping my depression.

Chapter 25

The Signs

In the meantime, some changes and unusual occurrences guided me to look into different spiritual paths, leading me toward a higher awakening of consciousness, and my writing reflected that. They were changing in accordance to my awakening process.

I was starting to detach from old paradigms, and the sense of freedom that I was slowly permitting myself to feel gave me a powerful sense of connection with the divine within me. One thing led to another, and many synchronicities was happening. I received messages from everywhere, which caught my attention through a high-pitched sound in my ears and head.

One day during a prayer I asked what the purpose of all this was. Soon after, I was guided to see a message on a spiritualist website that jumped off the screen, saying:

> When you speak in universal terms, energy forms are around the energy framework of those words, so always speak in a positive manner. There were only so many bodies that could fit on planet Earth at this exact time, and the reason you are here is because you have something important to give. So how do you find your inner beauty? How do

you take that next step? You help someone else find his or her beauty. You reflect it first and then learn how to be the light, because there are two ways of working with light: you can be the light, or you can reflect the light. Both are incredible gifts of light work on this planet.

Dear one, we see the struggles you go through. If it was possible for us to remove the veil for just a moment, for you to really see who you are, it would be magical and life would be easy for you.

Wow, that really made me shiver. It was too much of a "coincidence," and I know coincidences do not exist. They are actually unforeseen forces that work behind the scenes for things to happen to the right person at the right time and circumstances.

I wish I would have written down the name of the site, so I could thank them now. Those words instantly made me think of my old friend, the one who introduced me to Spiritism. She was always saying the same thing to me, with her own words, and on that day I got exactly the answers I needed, and a little more. I was learning to look for the signs but understood, then, that when life unfolds its trail within the unknown, the answers we pursue are in the simplest things within our being, and we must look within for those answers.

These synchronicities, epiphanies, and coincidences are common ground for those that are on their path of soul awakening, and those who have been through as I have will resonate with my experiences. I also knew that as the planet is currently undergoing a vibrational transformation to the higher vibratory energy level of love, this quantum leap in the evolution of the humankind, will propel a profound shift of our consciousness, to be experienced by those that are ready to get out of their current state of spiritual dormancy.

The negative events of my life were my wakeup call; most of the time, things need to be shifted around in order for us to see clearly who we are and what our purpose here is. Thus, the unplanned changes break the structures to give space for the real you. All has been a blessing in disguise. But I must add that a spiritual awakening is a personal journey in which there is no right and wrong, there is only individual experiences that elevate our way to see ourselves and the world around us.

I have noticed all different signs coming from diverse walks of life. I could not stop but to pay attention to the repetitive appearances of the numbers 11:11, 4:44, 5:55, 999, and so forth. They showed up everywhere I looked. Later I found out that this is the way the angels and archangels communicate with us.

Well, this went against everything I had learned. It was not easy to get rid of the feeling of unworthiness of attention from those higher beings, which have been inbuilt by some preconceived and misinterpreted ideas. What I knew about them was that those beings did not communicate directly with us but through our personal spiritual guide, due to our lower energy of frequency and vibrations -"Everything you see around you is vibrating at one frequency/energy speed or another, and so are you".

That made God, the Almighty, so untouchable. I certainly was not prepared for the other discoveries that were on the way. Another sign that did strike me was an increase in intuitive skill. I always have been an intuitive person, but now things were going beyond my imagination. I could even tell when people were lying.

My interests and likes were slowly changing, and I had a sense of urgency in learning more about this new path. I held a great desire to get a closer and more profound definition of the Creator, the universe, the world we live in, the reasons for our cosmic duality (positive-negative, right-wrong, yin-yang, female-male, good-bad, black-white, etc.); Which today I understand that are aspects absolutely necessary in the process of obtaining self-knowledge and for the evolution of the species.

I got an interest to learn more about the other living beings from our galaxy, and my connection with the whole. I could feel during meditation that there was no such a thing as separation, we are all beams of light shining through the darkness of life. In reality, we are simply the same divine light experiencing matter. Thus, we are all one.

My sense of responsibility grew deeper but in a more expanded, loving, and encompassing way. It was like I had a daily download of information that did not needed to be processed because I just easily understood. At some stage, I thought I was going crazy and imagining things. This was when the old self-doubts would come back to confuse me.

But I found out that there were many other people out there going through the same experiences. In one of those self-doubting moments, I heard a strong but calm voice saying,

> My dear friend and sister, touch the hearts of those who are in need of some words of compassion. Your strength surpasses the courage of a man in war, and I do not believe you understand the importance of your presence in the lives of those around you. I am here to say wake up and do it more. Inspire those without inspiration; spread those words across your universe; debase and break the rules of preconceived ideas and discriminations; relieve the pain and sorrow of those in search of truth.
>
> We are here to help you with this work. There are flowers blooming from the seeds you have unknowingly planted in the hearts and minds of many. You have reached people afar, and they

are praying for you to become closer to them. They pray for your work to spread.

Revolutionize those lives by exposing the beauty in its simplicity; be true to your self-beliefs, but in your conquest, make sure to abhor the ego; then provide food for the soul of many in need.

You are a light worker in the darkness of many souls, starting with your own son, who seeks your advice. He is a warrior and a light being who will find peace in equal rights. He will fight for liberty of thoughts; he is a warrior of peace; he will learn from you where to go, and he will conquer what he seeks.

Go ahead and enlighten the lives of many through your words, representing their truth in your behavior. Many look up to you, and many invisible friends will help you accomplish this mentoring and studying you need to acquire in order to subscribe to a life of loving service.

My intentions here are to give strength, support, and courage for you to pursue your life's purpose. Extend your universal mind to the world you can reach. We will do whatever is permitted by God to help you on this journey.

At this point I thought, *No way. This must be a mind trick, or some boisterous spirit playing with me.* Then, soon after, I clearly heard, "Believe it, but consult your conscience. You are not imagining all this. Life here is more real than you can comprehend. I am the flower that you touch, the smell in a breath of the ocean. I am the crystal that heals, the lucid imagination, the soil that fertilizes food, the grandness of life within—I am that, I am …"

That was way too powerful; I'd heard that expression before, "I am that, I am," through my studies of the Ascended Masters and the White Brotherhood, but I decided to put it aside for a while in order to logically process all that information that was directly related to me. I guess fear was my first reaction—we always fear the unknown.

Chapter 26

. . . .

Life's Parallels

Through self-searching I noticed that there is a great division inside us. There is a willingness to just be, to just stay, to change, or simply to leave it as is. And this inner ambiguity is portraying our will to a self-encounter. What psychologists call the inner finding, though I believe it goes beyond that. It is the unconscious inner call to our self-encounter with the whole. Our call to find what is our part to play and who is running the show.

It may be a call to God, nature, the Source, the universe, or unforeseen circumstances and strange forces that drive our lives like a runaway car. Deep down we are all in search of something to give meaning to our lives, or someone to lead us to discover that. Other times we just want to be left alone, with no interest or worries in knowing the truth.

Understanding the human mind has always been my fascination. It is one of the greatest enigmas, and we, the thinking beings of this planet, are all trying to use the art of good thinking, without really knowing how to control it. Isn't that ironic?

We all wish to be different sometimes: inconsequential, eloquent, irreverent, those so-called free behaviors that we see in youth, which we want to taste but fear to do so, as society would claim to be inconvenient, and even displeasing. Is that so? To me, there is a lack of light in what they see as normal, a lack of love in the love we see. Because what we see out there are imprisoned minds. Anything but love.

I see all of us as infinite light beings of this universe, but many today are mutants of their own wishes for being so involved in the overwhelming view of the masses. Why do we care so much about who is watching and what they think of us? We walk every step in this sad and painful reality, forcing social smiles, taking life as an apprentice of goodness, hoping to find happiness and learn how to live freely in the now. Free yourself from all this.

Today I picture life as a spark of the divine light experiencing matter. I will make a simple comparison and explain like this: The universe is a school, planet Earth is a classroom, the physical body is a school uniform, and our life is the school year.

So pay attention to the lessons presented in this classroom, study them, meditate on what you have learned, and put them into practice by helping those who are behind with their homework. Do not disturb others' learning path, invest in your daily self-improvement, and do not give up when facing the most difficult lessons. Take good care of your uniform, and do not disperse your attention with unproductive activities. Harmonize yourself with the other students, as the year goes by too fast, and thank the many teachers who crossed your path, assisting you with your divine ascension!

We all play a small but important part, a role in the grand picture of life. We are asked to fulfil our own individual parts and be attentive about when and how we can become a link to act upon and be at service. At this stage of life, we must go on with the show with our hearts and souls, having a clear conscience that we can only do our best with our current capabilities.

If in whatever situation you were unable to fulfil your part, rest assured that the role was not yours to be played. When this happens, there will always be someone else more capable of doing it to replace you. So do not worry when your attempts fail, as no one will be left behind without assistance. Do not get too involved in other people's problems either, because energetically, it can create links that carry loads that are not yours, shading and hindering your own path.

Our challenge in this play is to shine our light and being at service without getting too attached. Attachments bring heavy loads, so learn how to travel light throughout your life. Our main role is indeed to focus on our own path of evolution, not forgetting that the play has a higher purpose, and we are just working on a small portion of the big picture.

Chapter 27

Meditation as My Intimate Camino

One of the things that became vital to me during depression was meditation. Meditation is the harmonization of the physical and mental vibrations, which expands the level of consciousness. I was introduced to guided meditation through a dear friend, who was also on his own path of self-awakening. With a busy mind like mine, it took me quite a while to quiet it down. I found my own way through the breathing techniques, where I could start benefiting from this wonderful and most powerful way to seek inner peace.

Everyday afternoon I would find a nice place to seat comfortably, and started with a chakra cleansing guided meditation with Lilian Eden, via YouTube (Lilian Eden is an internationally respected, Spiritual Teacher/Advisor/Coach), who became my favourite meditation guide. I would like to thank her for guiding me out of depression.

I was so surprised to realize I needed to shut down all the thoughts that came through my head in order to clearly hear the inner voice that saved me from my own persona. Meditation works for me as a renewal tool of my energy level and a maintenance of calmness throughout the turmoil that I face in life.

I have never experimented with illicit drugs, but if I can compare anything to it, I believe meditation gives you that sensation of being high, but a much more powerful and meaningful high, as I can vividly touch this vibrant stillness that has opened doors I had never imagined. This was the missing key I needed in order to get in connection with the divine within.

Much to my delight, I found a new world in silence, and on those special time-out moments, all my worries would disappear. I saw everything in a much clearer way, as everything seemed to lose its importance compared to the majestic infinity of our true self and the insights we get from it. We are, in fact, the creators of our own reality.

When I thought at first that this was just my safe haven, I realized that is when heaven came to save me. Meditation was and is my intimate Camino (my path) toward my higher self and my integration with God's consciousness. I have fallen in love with it, and today it is my main source of self-discovery and equilibrium. In meditation I breathe, absorb, emanate, and live my prayers. The inspirations I get from it are amazing as after each meditation section, I am usually inspired to write, and when I read them out loud, I say, "Where all did this came from? How do I know all this? I was not thinking about that—who am I?"

Meditation is your tuning in with God, and intuition is God attuning with you. Silence your mind and listen!

Chapter 28

Creating Our Reality

The people we choose to have by our side play a great role in the successes or failures of our lives, and among them we find the ones who raise us, while others, even if subconsciously, will influence us with their fears, negativity, selfishness, insecurities, lack of faith, and lack of courage.

Those people may well be within our own family. So it is important to pay attention to it in order not to be negatively influenced by others' truths. Also, we should observe in our own actions the atavistic behaviors that are derived from self-limiting and destructive beliefs, ones that have been lived throughout time by everything we learned in childhood, consequently crystallizing all emotions related to those moments and impressing our subconscious with a false perception of a reality that has, over the years, hindered our full potential.

I was in this process of questioning and analyzing all past situations that may be currently inhibiting my possibilities to have, create, and attract new opportunities in my life. I could not understand that with such good experience and a strong resume, I was still not attracting any kind of a job.

The phrase "Our perceptions always become our reality" could not be more real. Those days have proven that my thoughts have power and were subconsciously attracting what I was believing.

Self-knowledge and self-control are paramount to challenge the pitfalls and identify beliefs that are responsible for the creations of self-sabotaging and illusory reality hidden in our subconscious. I was feeling an urgency and need of a mental-detox, to get rid of what was registered by my conscience and crystallized by my subconscious, so I could free myself from limitations that were imposed on me. I could not see then that life is filled with abundance and possibilities and is waiting for those who act without fear of failure or of rejection, as the impossible only exists for those who believes in it.

Be aware, as our minds exert great power materializing the reality that we create in the world we can see. It commands all of our actions, reactions, and decisions. We must reprogram our thoughts in order to attract success in all areas of our lives, as success is within the reach of all those who go beyond their self- limits, You can go as far as your mind allows you to go.

To help me with that, I discovered affirmations - "Affirmations are positive, specific statements that help you to overcome self-sabotaging, negative thoughts".(Wikipedia).

Believing or having faith is the key to all manifestations, (positive and negative), which works in perfect harmony with the law of attraction. You will attract what you believe. Our minds are programmed to easily focus on the negative aspects of life. Positive affirmations, helps to send positive messages to the sub-conscience and consequently re-program your mind to respond in a positive way. I focused on them every time I meditated. They strengthened my hope for change.

Another thing that got clear in my mind is that it is important to not let others' opinions, or even the misunderstood child within, sabotage our ideals with the false pretense of protecting itself from an alleged pain. This process of sabotage was falsely created by unresolved emotions from past events, due to a lack of full view and understanding of the truth.

I fell into this trap, never able to finish anything or believe I could. Everything I started in my life I left halfway done, always procrastinating anything important. Procrastination has a lot to do with the fear of facing possible difficulties along the way. But being in command of the events of my life and being able to focus and affirm on what is positive was essential to reprogramming my mind.

Through my meditation states, I could look at the big picture and realize that we are all an important and integral part of this cosmic engineering that acts precisely, so nature can lead us to the fulfilment of a larger plan.

The days went by with no return, and we should not waste any time whining or becoming a victim of circumstances.

Remember, the only approval we need in order to follow our own aspirations is from our own conscience. If we align our thoughts with beauty and goodness, with what brings inner happiness, and with what encourages us to go beyond our own barriers, we will comprehend that the truth lies within and cannot be found elsewhere.

You are exactly at the point and place where your choices or lack of courage to make them has put you. But you deserve to achieve what you wish, without fear, without guilt or feelings of inferiority, because the sky is not a limit for a humanity who was created by an unlimited creator!

In summary, the purpose of our lives is to allow our divine essence to express itself and evolve through its experiences. Our outer world will then inevitably always be the reflection of what is inside. So, project it out to the best of your ability, and eliminate the mental toxins that are programmed to hinder your footsteps.

Chapter 29

....

Reality Check

More than six months had passed, and I had a few phone calls showing interest in my skills, but I went on only three interviews. My money was running out, and when my bank account was left with just enough to pay my mortgage the following month, my son came to me and said, "Mom, aren't you worried? Things are getting bad, and we may have to sell what's left—our home. But I don't see you concerned; you seem way too calm for someone who may lose her home."

Yes, I was concerned, but I refused to lose my hair and my health over this. Maybe I was overwhelmed, and that was my way of shutting down and protecting my mental health. It was then that I notice that meditation was helping me stay calm and centered during this difficult phase.

If I stopped to think, I would find that life had a harsh way of proving its point to me. Firstly, my relationship—gone; then, my womanhood issue—gone (that was positive); then my job— gone (today I see that was positive too); then my volunteer work at a spiritual centre—gone. Would detachment also mean that my home would soon be gone?

I did not want to think about it, as the thought of it upset my stomach. It gave me a feeling of total failure. This place meant a lot to my son and me. We moved here after my divorce to his father, and this was where I raised him by myself.

I have no family in Australia, so once I got my divorce payout, I decided to make sacrifices and bite a bigger piece of the apple than I could chew. I bought my mom's home and then I bought our apartment. I had no cash, no backup money, and a huge mortgage. The main reason I did that was so I could stay closer to work and to my friend, who was like a mother to me. Also, the apartment was located in a closed and secured complex. It made me feel safe when leaving my son home alone after school. All worked out perfectly; this place was right close to my work and his primary school at that time.

Yes, the mortgage was high for me, but I felt I could give him a better and safer home there. It was indeed our safe haven. It was the only material investment I had. I was never good with saving money, but I was good at paying my debts; back then I did not earn enough to save anyway, as I could barely make ends meet. About six years earlier I had lost a nice property in Brazil, that I have bought for investment. It was part of my retirement plan, an apartment in front of the beach, in the town I was born. The payments got too high, as the interest rates in Brazil are huge. I was then unable to meet both properties payments at the same time, leaving with me no other option but to sell it. So to think that I could lose our safe haven was way too hard to swallow.

I knew that a decision would have to be made sooner or later if I did not find a job before I ran out of money. So I was biding my time, applying for jobs, negotiating my debts with the banks, cutting down on costs by cancelling my health coverage and home insurance, and applying for hardship assistance with my two credit card accounts and with the government.

I even thought of moving into a friend's place, to rent a room and then lease my home, but my son's income was not enough to pay for both of us. Renting my home would cover its own debt but not the strata levies, council rates, and other expenses. If I went to the government and asked for support, the amount they would give me would not be enough to cover it all, and if I rented out my home, they would stop the payments. Catch twenty-two.

I was trying my best to buy time and save my home, but I could not hold out any longer. I gave myself until the end of the month to decide, and I had only thirteen days left. I was praying every day for a miracle, but nothing happened, so I decided to get help from the government—and guess what? They refused to help me, because they asked me to call back my last job, and find out the brake up of my payout, so they could calculate how much they would give me. When I have already provided them with all necessary information to calculate that themselves without putting me into the humiliating position of going back to that place, where I was badly treated for years. That was my last chance to keep my home. All those closed doors were pushing me into a direction that I did not wish to follow. Now I was in big trouble, but something had to be done.

In the meanwhile, creativity played a great part as self-therapy. In order to get some cash, better than nothing, my friend and I decided to use our creativity and create glamorous ornaments to sell at the markets. Making those ornaments took hours, but they really turned out gorgeous and gave us a sense of direction. The time we spent creating them were real therapy sessions, as we laughed and chatted all day long. Working with our hands in a creative way makes wonders for the soul.

Our first day at the church market was not successful, so we thought about making an online business, as those ornaments used to take quite a long time to be completed, plus we did not have enough stock for bigger and more prestigious arts and crafts types of markets. I felt quite proud when my most beautiful creation was sold on the first day. It gave me some hope, but at the end of the day, we both left there a little disappointed. Reality really checked!

I have some Doreen Virtue angels cards (Doreen is an

American author and founder of Angel Therapy, a type of New Age therapy based on the premise that communicating with angels is the key to healing), which I used everyday to get some motivating messages from above. On the next day of the market, after a prayer, I decided to take one of the cards. It said, "Make a decision and do not look back, because you are protected by the angels."

I had been crying myself to sleep nearly every day, and one morning after my meditation I was inspired to automatically write/psychograph a message from my spiritual guide, and she said:

> Why do you weep, if you know that none of this will be taken with you? Today this house shelters you, protects you, tomorrow another house will home you. Why are you crying when you do not live in pities, and the bread has never left your table? You have the support of loyal old friends, and the prayer of thy mother that cries out for you. You know that you will lack nothing, as you know well of the lessons to learn with this. There is only suffering when you resist, so make your decision confidently, because even though, my daughter, you have distanced yourself, your essence calls me.
>
> I hear your crying for help and I wrap you in light, and you fall asleep in deaf ears. Why are you crying when you know the reality of things? For your happiness will not take long to arrive. Wait with confidence and patience, because the tonic of life will revive you from grief.
>
> Bless the divine gifts that surround you and the many brothers who hold affection for you. Cherish gratitude in your heart and continue your life with no regrets. Do not worry much about

tomorrow, or what has passed; live as if today
was your last day on the divine mother earth,
which warms you with so much love.

Heaven knows how much I needed to hear that. I guess
guardian angels can be quite harsh and direct, but I guess
that's their job, right?

Chapter 30

On the Road to Soul Recovery

In spite of all the pressure, I had a feeling that I was on the right track toward the road of my soul recovery and that something would happen to change things around. That inner faith, in times of sorrow, we do not know where it comes from. So another message came to save the day:

> Everything will change, because everything changes. Believe me, your life will not be the same anymore. It's time to do what you came here to practice. The negative roadblocks that were hindering this moment of light have been removed from your path of elevation and work for goodness. Until this date, everything was only an exercise in relation to spirituality. Your destination, which was outlined in pre-uterine epochs, is about to start, and a new life dawned in the coming days. Continue your path with confidence, because the worst is behind. This is the last door to be closed, because many others will open. Do not think that it will be easy, but everything will be done at ease, because the student is now ready to be a master once again.

We, the invisible friends, are working behind the scenes so that everything goes as planned. Do not blame yourself for your negative thoughts, they are effects of the flesh in which you find yourself at the moment and of the surrounding vibrations, but you will be much help to a lot of people. Your friend is right, all of you are united by a divine reason, and the future is of light, success, and happiness, much joy. Congratulations. You have conquered your own self.

When I read this message, a million thoughts passed, and I could see that selling my apartment was another lesson, a lesson of material detachment, and that was a hard one. *Really, do I have to?* I questioned. But the answer was clear.

With no money left, and the banks calling to advise me that my time was up, I had no other choice but to sell my apartment. That hurt—oh, that hurt a lot. So I called a friend of mine, who worked as a real estate agent, and asked him to put the place on the market right away. I cried myself to sleep that night.

However, as soon as the decision was made, I started receiving phone calls for interviews. All of them were for positions paying much less than what I used to get from the bank. Positions from past experiences, but I was in no financial luxury to pick and choose, so I went to all of them. Although I gave my best shot, my self-esteem was so low that even for something I knew I could do with my eyes shut, I left the interview feeling hopeless.

What a horrible feeling it was getting into those office environments. It gave me a bad sense of déjà vu. I guess this was all the mental toxins from my previous work experiences, which I needed to shake off.

The more interviews I attended, the more confident I got. I could see light at the end of that tunnel and was losing weight, getting out of the house more, cleaning the clutter, moving the energy around. This simple act helped me get a clear vision of a new horizon and shifted me to respond to what was happening in my life. I understood that I had to depart from that place that held so many memories of my single mom's life, because it was time for it.

The house opening started, and I was trying to start my detachment process with it. It was not easy. I felt like a failure, and every time the real estate agent would come back with negative feedback, my hope of a debt-free life vanished. But I fought that, and tried to keep my faith by saying, "God, I am here doing my part, so please give me a positive sign. Okay, detachment. I got the message now. Please don't leave me alone."

That was a tough lesson for not being mindful of my money. I would never be in that position if I knew how to use what I got in a more responsible and careful way. Would I ever learn that? I am still coming to terms with that.

Nearly tree weeks with the property on the market, and I finally got a phone call from the real estate agent saying that it was sold for more than I expected. I signed the contracts with a tight but at the same time relieved heart.

As everything in my life is not standard, I signed the contracts over to the new owner in the morning of that day, and guess what? I received a job offer. At the time, I sincerely did not know if I should cry of happiness or sadness, thinking if the phone calls had been received the other way around, I would not have sold my home.

Oh well, I will always take that as a sign that it was meant to be. Now it was just a matter of going through the worst job in life, moving out.

I found a new and beautiful place to rent in nearby suburb, and after a month I started a brand-new life: new home, new job, newly fresh and positive mind set.

I thought this was the hardest detachment lesson I have ever had to go through, because it involved the security I wanted to give my son, so I said to my friends and family, "I'm not afraid of anything anymore. God has tested my faith and strength a lot the past two years. I guess I have learned great lessons and probably paid some karmic debts, but please, Lord, spare me anything else. I am strong and know I can go through a lot (except losing someone dear). Forgive me now what I am going to say: I am really tired of all this. Lord, I am tired, please spare me. I am not sure if I can handle anything else, and emotionally I am a wreck!"

Chapter 31

. . . .

New Home, New Job, New Life

The new year was exciting, and I had 365 days ahead of infinite possibilities. I felt on the top of the world in spite of all the losses. Refreshed in my overall beliefs, I took all on the chin and thanked God every day to have helped me come out of that life turmoil in a sane and positive state of mind, and for having given me a new opportunity.

I was still sensitive to bad news, so I tried to make my life as easy and simple as possible. I accepted an easy job, earning way less than before. It was nothing like what I was doing previously. In fact, I think I was trying to run away from the corporate world because I was still burned out. This time I was managing a small administration team in an aggregator company, with wonderful and relaxed bosses.

I must admit that it was hard to adapt down in processes and procedures. The place was a start-up company with no established set of rules and procedures, and for me, who came from a corporate world, it took a while to put everything in place to then feel at home. I used my skills to help them organize my department, as they were going through a further development process. For me it was a walk in the park, and for that I thanked God every day.

Everything was going smoothly, and I confess I felt scared

about that. When you go through so many hardships, and then everything seems to go well, you feel suspicious. But I felt that I deserved that break. It was sounding like a happy end, right? I thought I deserved that.

After seven months I took three weeks off to go to my cousin's wedding in Europe. It was a family reunion overseas that the whole family was so much looking forward to. From Brazil, my mother, grandmother, aunty, nephew, and cousins and their partners went, and from New Zealand and Australia my other aunty and I came. We all met in Germany, where our other part of the family lives, and from there we all travelled to Munich and then to our main destination, Croatia, where the wedding took place. Croatia is an amazing place. I loved it, and the wedding was unforgettable. Who would think that my family and I would one day meet and travel together through Europe?

The whole family stayed in Europe for three weeks, though my mother, grandmother, and aunty stayed in Germany for another two weeks. They had the time of their lives. And after so much suffering that those warriors women endured through their life time, they deserved that special holiday.

Chapter 32

The Hardest Detachment There Is

Back from Europe, that old question came to play in my mind: "Why does everything that is good end so fast?" Little did I know that I was about to endure the toughest lesson ever.

Returning to work after a holiday is always so hard, is it not? I started my routine feeling melancholic. I was already missing everyone and what I had lived. Everything had left me with a taste of gratitude, but, strangely enough, also with a fear in my heart. I guess it was due to have gone through so much on the past years. I could not believe I'd had such a wonderful trip with my family.

I did not know how to handle happiness. That was something that I would never think I could ever be able to afford to do. I was so glad to see everyone together and happy. But that did not last long. On the same week I arrived from Europe, destiny came to test my strength once again.

My middle brother, who was in Brazil and had gone through a great trial in his life for years with depression, was finally showing signs of coming out of the dark night of the soul; although he was feeling happier at that time (at least that was what he externally was showing), he went through five cardiac arrests and was in coma.

Although one of my cousins was able to bring him back to life with CPR after the first heart attack, on the way to the hospital he suffered a consecutive fourth heart attack, having to immediately be put into an induced coma.

I prayed: "Oh dear Lord, I have asked you to spare me. I was not ready for that."

As soon as my sister-in-law called my younger brother, who lives in New Zealand, and me to tell us our brother was in coma, and with little chance to survive, and that only a miracle would bring him back, we decided to go to Brazil together the following morning.

I was in total shock but had to act fast, as we had not much time left. I rang my boss in tears on that horrible Sunday night and told him what had happened. I told him that I needed to be by my mother's side at that time, so I was going to Brazil the following morning. Luckily he was nice enough to support me through this.

I could not describe what I was feeling. My world was collapsing. My middle brother in a coma? I could not believe it! It sounded like I was living a horror movie. I could not think properly but had to be at the airport at five in the morning. It was nearly three a.m. and I still had not managed to pack my bags. I was acting like a crazy person, crying, shaking, walking up and down talking to myself, trying to keep calm. I was extremely nervous, confused, and in disbelief.

Various little movies of our lives, our childhood, our regular weekend of philosophical conversations over Skype came to play in my mind. But all I could do was ask God to have mercy and keep him alive, to allow us to see our loving brother again, to hear his voice, his funny jokes, to give him a hug and say, "Mano, I love you." I asked God for strength because I knew that my mother would be devastated and would need my support.

That was the longest and saddest trip back home ever. I could not believe that both of us were travelling to Brazil on that Monday, but this time, not for a happy holiday. A weekend earlier I had just arrived from the best trip of my life. One day you laugh; others you cry—is that how it's supposed to be?

This was one of the worst experiences of my life. I was always strong about anything, and although I am someone with a lot of spiritual knowledge, I wasn't ready to lose someone dear.

Those that are close to me have heard me saying over and over again, "After going through what I went through last year, nothing scares me anymore. But one thing is for sure, spare me, Lord, of losing someone dear. I cannot handle that." I wonder if I was having a premonition.

When my father passed away five years ago, it was sad, but we did not have a close relationship, so I was able to handle it better. But this time, God, you came too close to my heart. I remember it like it was today, and even now when I am writing these words, I am reliving those days. I cannot help but cry. It is still way too hard to grasp this new reality.

We arrived in Brazil on the afternoon of that same day, as we were going back thirteen hours in time. However, unfortunately, the hospital visiting time was over for that day. There was no good news for my brother; he was still in coma, not responding to any test or medication.

The whole family got together at my grandmother's house and spent time in constant prayer. My young brother and I could not wait to get to the hospital the next morning.

My family is usually a happy, party-hearty kind of family, but this was the first time I saw every single one in their own little corner, crying, praying for my brother's life. My brother was always the light of the party, the helping hand, the caring one, always made us laugh, and now there we were, under one roof, united yes, but this time in tears and fear for his life. The one who took care of everyone else forgot to take care of himself.

Looking into my mother's eyes, I had to pull out from my soul the last strength I had. I am also a mother and could not help but put myself in her shoes. I saw the pain in her eyes and

I doubly suffered in silence. Mum was glad that we were both there during the toughest time of her life. We made the right decision.

On the following morning we returned to the hospital, and we could not believe what we saw. It was a shock to see our loving brother intubated like that, supported by machines.

The doctor took all of our hopes away when he said, "Only God can help now. We have tried everything, and he is not responding. If he wakes up, he will live in a vegetative state." Nonetheless, we still had the hope of the greatest Doctor of all, Jesus Christ. We all prayed for a miracle.

My mother did not want to go to the hospital; she could not handle seeing him like that again. Getting back to Mum after our hospital visit was hard. I did not have the courage to repeat what the doctor had mentioned. It was way too heartbreaking to take away her hopes, so I just said, "The doctors said that nothing has changed."

I held my tears, and after speaking to her, I excused myself and ran to the bathroom, away from everyone. There I fell on my knees, tears pouring down, and talked to God. I asked my guides for spiritual intervention. I asked Mother Mary to have mercy on his soul. I asked her to please look after my brother, to please either bring him back to us healthy with no sequelae, or have mercy and take him away, but please to not let him come back and live in a vegetative state, as he did not deserve that.

As soon as I asked for that, I felt a hand on my shoulder. A female voice said, "Daughter, do not despair, he is already with us, we will look after him. The last thing to detach is the heart life string, and soon all will be over." That gave me some relief, and somehow that kind and loving voice sort of put me to sleep.

After that, I managed to take a little nap in my grandmother's lounge. I was waiting for the next hospital visiting time on that same night. We wanted to be there every day, until he woke up. Hope is the last feeling to die.

There were people from all over the world, from all types

of faiths praying for him. In our family, there are Protestants, Catholics, and Spiritists, and every one of us were united in one heart.

As soon as I fell asleep, something extraordinary happened. I saw myself out of my body, and was automatically pulled toward the kitchen door. I then saw my mother crying. She was sitting at the kitchen table, head down, and I could hear her thoughts. Mom was praying, conversing with my brother, and in her thoughts, she was saying, "Son, please wake up. Where are you, son? Come back home. Come back to me."

Then, immediately after she said that, I saw my brother's spirit outside the kitchen door, and he said, "I am here, Mom. Mom, I'm here!"

It was so vivid, so real, that I instantly woke up scared. I asked my cousin if my sister-in-law went to the hospital. Minutes later the hospital rang, asking someone from the family to go over there. My heart jumped. I was shaking as my dream came to my mind, and I remembered the voice that I'd heard in the bathroom. Although until the end I hoped that the hospital was calling to say that he'd woken from the coma, I knew he was gone.

I thought, *They heard my prayers. My brother was taken away.* I received a text message from a friend confirming that my brother had passed away.

What I went through during that night and days to come, I do not wish on anyone. It was horrible. I had to be the strong pillar to all. To physically detach from someone that I love is the hardest and saddest thing I ever had to go through. He had left us one day after we arrived in Brazil, and I will never forget that day. The eighteenth of August, the same date of my arrival in Australia twenty-three years ago.

The funeral was so beautiful, and so many people came to pay their respects and show solidarity with our family. People I had not seen since my childhood were there. I think he was the only one that did not realize how important he was to us and loved by all.

Every single one that would get close to his coffin remembered some good deed. Even his bosses were there, very sad. My brother was someone that I had admired all my life. He was an extremely intelligent and handsome man of a kind, humble, lonely, and misunderstood soul, with a heart of gold, a heart that I love so much and miss dearly. But I know now that God takes the good ones away earlier, at the height of their vitality, so their sudden absence draws attention to the values they exemplified in their short existence.

Thank God for my psychic abilities, because since then my brother has reached out to me. I can feel his presence sometimes, and for many of my family members, he has appeared in their dreams. In all of them he is well and says that he is happy in spite of missing his children, Mom, and all of us. He is in a good place.

To each family member was a hidden lesson in all this, each in their unique ways. My brother taught me the greatest and toughest detachment lesson of my life: Do not ever take for granted the people in your life; do not ever take for granted your strength; do not ever take for granted the little signs of loneliness someone near is giving; do not ever take for granted life itself; do not ever give too much importance to the material matters of life; do not ever forget to love without expectations. Life is a fragile thread that can be broken when you least expect it, and getting attached to anything that may hinder your soul evolution is a tough illusion to free yourself from.

I became strong and fearless, but contradictorily, deep down I was still fragile and tired by all the lessons I had to endure. Today, I can see that insecurities and the fear of unforeseen changes come from our lack of ability to focus on the blessings that those same difficulties can bring to our own soul.

An awakened and courageous soul is not afraid of the new, not afraid to change the script of their lives, not afraid to face any challenges that may bring the necessary inner reform to eliminate the old way of thinking, acting, and reacting toward all which has kept their growth in a stationary state. Most of us live in a state of subconsciousness to the blessings of the present moment.

Life goes on, on both sides, and love never dies. The understanding of this sublime but powerful reality keeps us involved in strong connections. It is important to remember that we are not the physical body that we see in the mirror; we are here temporarily and for the evolution of our spirit.

The departure of my brother still hurts, his physical absence hurts, but I can feel his loving presence. With that I learned that an extended suffering from the loss of a loved one defines our resistance to acceptance, to the emptiness and incompleteness left by the absence of those who departed earlier than us.

Each elevated thought in prayer, in happy memories, and in sending love vibrations will be received as happy balms of light and peace by those in other realms, thus fulfilling the great purpose of interconnecting on the same intimate wavelength of feelings and thoughts during the momentary physical separation.

If we suffer, they suffer too. Tears of anger and anguish unbalance the mind and the heart and express a lack of faith in the designs of the Creator. If we rejoice, they will rejoice also. The tears of longing express love and happy memories, bringing up the same smile of yesterday.

The departed ones did not die, they only fulfilled the time determined for their development on earth, transforming itself. It was not a goodbye but a see you later, because one day all of us will reunite again.

After all, we are not human beings having a spiritual experience. We are spiritual beings having a human experience.

Thank you, my dear, loving brother. I feel that with your departure, a part of me has died—the old part of me. As like a phoenix, always rising from the ashes, so did I. See you one day in heaven.

Chapter 33

A Message from Above

I want to end this book with a message that summarizes my journey until this point and with the hope it will touch the heart of many of you. This message I received from a spiritual friend:

> To the proportions and extent of its consciousness, the human being will expand its perception of what they are, where they came from, and what their purpose is, thus fulfilling its integral role in the creation of the world, as co-creators. While stuck in materiality of all aspects, they will have difficulty lifting the veil of darkness that blinds them to the path they should take toward the light, lying cloudy, in front of their sleeping souls.
>
> The setbacks they face are creations of the mind. The mind expels them as reflections of itself, for matter of regaining balance and re-energizing the scattered forces which were used in the opposite directions to their redemption path, of the purification of the soul, of salvation, of evolution, or return to Source—call it as you may.

All are being called. Many feel an intimate dissatisfaction, but certainly not all of them are listening. Some confuse the message for allegories, others are taking every single word by the books. It is necessary to expand the vision, be open to the new, to what their limited mind sees as impossible and unacceptable; Only then, they will take a quantum leap in evolution and in understanding of their own origin and role within the whole.

The student should not give up the lesson by finding it difficult to understand. It is this information, integrated with the universal love that comes from the Source, that will pave the way to self-enlightenment, as told by master Buddha. Raise the flag of love thy neighbor, as also taught by the Prince of Peace, Jesus; and see the other as part of God's oneness, as beings in their ascension path toward the great intelligence that governs everything.

For humanity, within its present level of vibration, the spirituality in general seems to be all subtle, but its in fact by becoming subtle that they will clearly realize its real essence. Believe it! Just by your awakened presence on the planet at this moment, all of you are like open paths, for those who are thirsty for knowledge and for those who desire to change the not-so-picturesque frame, which is made before their earthly eyes. However, while they may only perceive sorrow and pain, for us everything is running as planned.

The light is present and strong in every being in the care of our observant eyes. We are sheltering and embracing the awakened one, those who are in their self-searching process, so they can fulfil their mission in favor of the others, the sleeping souls of this beautiful blue planet.

Strength, perseverance, joy, courage, and faith.

Now and forever … A friend!

Chapter 34

Final Word from the Author

Do not resist, learn to let it go as fast as you can, because life will work in a way that if it must be, it will take it from you anyway. Nonetheless, do not despair when the storm is passing by, as it came to transform you, to change you for the best you can be.

Those storms will bring in the new and make us see life with renewed perspectives, thus teaching us to release the old, unresolved emotions and learn the lessons of detachments. When all is settled, you'll look back and notice how much you grew with it. But in order to do so, you must forgive everything that has happened.

There are some things that happen to us in life where we sometimes will doubt the existence of a divine goodness. That is because life tends to give us the experiences we need in order to become stronger.

I have learned then that I wasn't a victim but a co-participant of the situations of my life. I have learned to have no expectations, because we will always get hurt.

I have learned that self-knowledge helped me to love others in an intense and detached way. I have learned that to forgive people when they hurt us, we must try to see the world from their point of view. They are also in search of their own happiness.

Each and every one of us are on a path of evolution and growth, and we can only offer what we have to give. I also learned that I was entirely responsible for my thoughts and what they have created, and only by comprehending how this cosmic engineer works can I see how I can forgive what I thought was unjust and unforgivable.

If you permit, you will also comprehend that nothing is by chance, and everything has a higher reason to be. Look for happiness within yourself, because that's where happiness lives. However, if you allow your feelings to get attached to things or people, you will always be vulnerable to their vulnerabilities.

Remember, everything works in our favor. What we think of as bad most often are blessings in disguise.

May the divine light that resides within your soul awaken the most sublime beauty and love of your being, and you will become light in the life of those who surround you every day!